StyleCity

BERLIN

StyleCity

BERLIN

With over 400 colour photographs and 5 maps

Thames & Hudson

Contents

Series concept and editor: Lucas Dietrich
Jacket and book design: Grade Design Consultants
Original design and map concept: The Senate
Maps: Peter Bull

Research and texts: Siân Tichař & Nils Peters
Specially commissioned photography by
Robert Lyons except:

Courtesy Engelbrecht: p. 139 (left)
Ralf Feldmeier: p. 134 (left), p. 137
Courtesy Savoy Hotel: p. 132
Dirk Schaper: pp. 120–21

Although every effort has been made to ensure that the information in this book is as up-to-date and as accurate as possible at the time of going to press, some details are liable to change.

First published in the United Kingdom in 2004 by
Thames & Hudson Ltd, 181A High Holborn,
London WC1V 7QX

www.thamesandhudson.com

British Library Cataloguing-in-Publication Data
A catalogue record for this book is available from the British Library

ISBN 0-500-21012-8

Printed in China

How to Use This Guide

The book features two principal sections: **Street Wise** and **Style Traveller**.

Street Wise, which is arranged by neighbourhood, features areas that can be covered in a day (and night) on foot and includes a variety of locations – cafés, shops, restaurants, museums, performance spaces, bars – that capture local flavour or are lesser-known destinations.

The establishments in the **Style Traveller** section represent the city's best and most characteristic locations – 'worth a detour' – and feature hotels (**sleep**), restaurants (**eat**), cafés and bars (**drink**), boutiques and shops (**shop**) and getaways (**retreat**).

Each location is shown as a circled number on the relevant neighbourhood map, which is intended to provide a rough idea of location and proximity to major sights and landmarks rather than precise position. Locations in each neighbourhood are presented sequentially by map number. Each entry in the **Style Traveller** has two numbers: the top one refers to the page number of the neighbourhood map on which it appears; the second number is its location.

For example, the visitor might begin by selecting a hotel from the **Style Traveller** section. Upon arrival, **Street Wise** might lead him to the best joint for coffee before guiding him to a house-museum nearby. After lunch he might go to find a special jewelry store listed in the **shop** section. For a memorable dining experience, he might consult his neighbourhood section to find the nearest restaurant cross-referenced to **eat** in **Style Traveller**.

Street addresses are given in each entry, and complete information – including email and web addresses – is listed in the alphabetical **contact** section. Travel and contact details for the destinations in **retreat** are given at the end of **contact**.

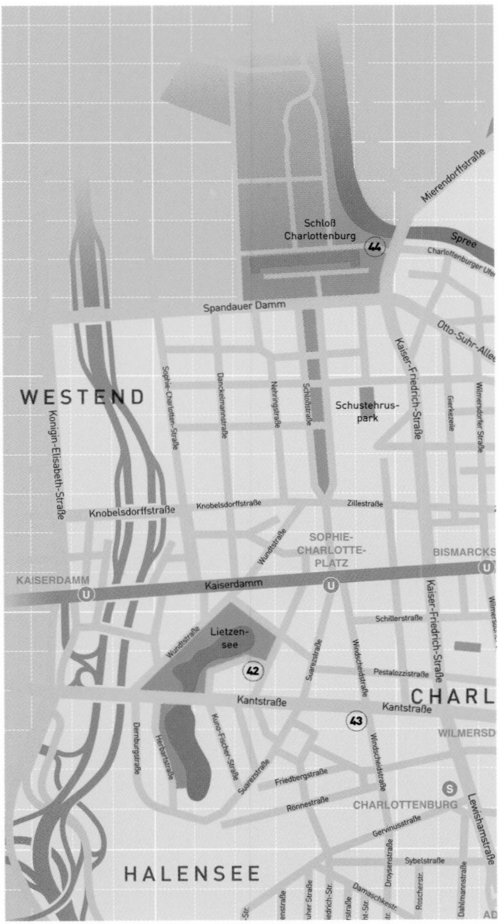

Legend

2 Location

Museums, sights

Gardens, squares

U S U-Bahn and S-Bahn stations

Streets

BERLIN

Among the great European capitals Berlin stands apart in its embodiment of an exhilarating, inspiring and often chaotic central European history and culture. It is a city of extremes in which, over the past two centuries, arts, culture and world politics have merged as a unique urban construct. Its erratic development through phases of accelerated intellectual and cultural growth, alternating with plateaus of consolidating creativity, is crucial to the metropolis's socio-political shaping and provides a bridge of understanding over the German–Slav divide.

Once a tranquil medieval 'double' city consisting of Berlin and Cölln, the city became the seat of the powerful Hohenzollern family in the 15th century and later the capital of Prussia, a kingdom with a legendary royal lineage leading to Friedrich the Great. Occupied by Napoleon's army from 1806 to 1808, Berlin became capital of the German Reich in 1871, played host to Germany's development into an industrialized and militarized country under Otto von Bismarck, experienced acutely the First World War, lived the 'Golden 1920s', endured the financial crash in the Weimar Republic, witnessed the rise of the Nazis and their complete defeat and the destruction of an entire nation in 1945, was cleaved in two between 1961 and 1989 then reunified when the infamous Wall came down and the German government was restored. Today, quite frankly, the city is one of the most exciting places in Europe, a cultural force to be reckoned with and a global player.

Through centuries of resisting new orders and regimes, Berlin has reacted with a subversive and often harsh irony, establishing a *Weltanschauung* (world view) that teeters between ideology and pragmatism. Nowhere else in Europe can such contradictory intellectual, cultural and political tensions be felt and experienced so vividly or have given rise to such a rich variety of urban life, generated not just by the affairs of state but by the assimilation of countless artistic enterprises and scientific discoveries. Charlottenburg Castle (p. 103), the Staatsratsgebäude of the former Communist government, the vast empty space of the once impressive Hohenzollern castle and the new Kanzleramt all stand as potent reminders of former kingdoms and political systems. Although the city suffered endless foreign occupations and rule by governments just and unjust, there was always inspiration to fuel the fascinating richness of its cultural achievements. The Museumsinsel (p. 17), now part of UNESCO's World Cultural Heritage programme, the Staatsoper, the Komische Oper, the Deutsche Oper, the Philharmonie (p. 41) and Bertolt Brecht's theatre, the

Berliner Ensemble (p.36), are all testimony to the city's deep-seated cultural involvement and pride.

But perhaps even more inspiring today is the explosive creativity of the small-scale, informal artistic undertakings of designers, musicians, architects and artists that have flourished in the city's former eastern sections, Mitte and Prenzlauer Berg. The creative atmosphere here is inspired not only by art-historical precedents such as Expressionism, which can be found at the Brücke Museum (p.176) or the Bauhausarchiv, but by the edginess and inventiveness of Berlin's underground scene, which has long attracted young artists from around the world. Here new trends and fashions are incubated in an urban laboratory uncontaminated by mainstream culture.

The quiet, leafy, former western neighbourhoods have also been caught up in the hectic reshaping of the city that took place after 1989, but they remain altogether more comfortable. Charlottenburg, Wilmersdorf and Grunewald exhibit the stately lifestyle of the middle and upper classes, with beautiful Art Déco quarters, impressive villas and affluent places to live and work dating from the turn of the last century. Cutting through them is the main shopping avenue, the Kurfürstendamm, which despite its touristic feel is lined with large, elegant stores that conceal secrets tucked away in neighbouring streets and squares. The cultural heart of Berlin extends to its surroundings, which have evolved into destinations of great interest. The entire city of Potsdam, once the imperial capital of Brandenburg and official residence of the Hohenzollerns, is listed as a World Cultural Heritage site and today the place represents a pleasing but heady mix of independent tastes and styles.

The political changes of 1989 led to an enormous enterprise: the physical and social reunification of more than 3.5 million people, divided by a wall but united by a complex and tumultuous history. New urban areas, such as Potsdamer Platz or the government district, are reminders of Berlin's unceasing commitment to rehabilitating itself and to healing the wounds of repeated incursions and depredations. Visitors experience a genuinely fresh urban perspective, made tangible in ambitious architectural projects that rival those of other great cities. Yet Berlin's essential beauty lies in its secluded ambience, palpable, perhaps, in its desire to preserve a slower, more intellectual lifestyle. The condition of a more secluded European metropolis away from the mainstream tourist, politicians' and financiers' tracks has in turn given birth to new attitudes towards design, architecture and lifestyle that permeate the many layers – some more apparent than others – of this unforgettable city.

Street Wise

Mitte • Potsdamer Platz • Kreuzberg • Friedrichshain • Prenzlauer Berg • Schöneberg • Tiergarten • Charlottenburg • Wilmersdorf

MS

Mitte
Potsdamer Platz

WEDDING
PRENZLAUER BERG
EBERSWALDER STRASSE
Danziger Straße
REINICKENDORFER STRASSE
SCHWARTZKOPFFSTRASSE
Sellerstraße
Boyenstraße
Chausseestraße
Heidestraße
Scharnhorststraße
Habersaathstraße
ZINNOWITZER STRASSE
NORDBAHNHOF
Invalidenstraße
Invalidenstr.
Veteranenstraße
Volkspark am Weinberg
Brunnenstr.
ROSENTHALER PLATZ
Torstraße
Rosenthaler Straße
Kastanienallee
Oderberger Str.
Schönhauser Allee
Kollwitzstraße
Sredzkistr.
Wörther Straße
Knaackstraße
Prenzlauer Allee
SENEFELDERPLATZ
Senefelder-platz
Metzer Straße
Saarbrücker Straße
Schwedter Straße
Fehrbelliner Str.
Zehdenicker Str.
Lottumstraße
Christinenstr.
Choriner Straße
Strassburger Str.
Linienstraße
Mulackstraße
Steinstraße
Gipsstraße
Sophienstr.
Auguststraße
Große Hamburger Straße
Kl. Hamburger Str.
ROSA-LUXEMBURG-PLATZ
Weydinger Str.
Hirtenstr.
Almstadtstraße
Mollstraße
WEINMEISTER-STRASSE
Weinmeisterstr.
Münzstraße
Karl-Liebknecht-Straße
Memhardstr.
Karl-Marx-Allee
Berolinastraße
SCHILLINGSTRASSE
Jacobystraße
Neue Blumenstraße
ORANIENBURGER TOR
ORANIENBURGER STRASSE
Oranienburger Straße
Krausnickstr.
Tucholskystraße
Friedrichstraße
Hannoversche Straße
Ziegelstraße
Reinhardtstraße
Schumannstr.
Albrechtstraße
Luisenstraße
Alexanderufer
Unterbaumstraße
Ludwig-Erhard-Ufer
Willy-Brandt-Str.
Bismarck Str.
Schiffbauerdamm
Marienstraße
Am Weidendamm
Monbijou-park
Bode-museum
Pergamon-museum
Alte Nationalgalerie
Neues Museum
Altes Museum
Berliner Dom
HACKESCHER MARKT
Dircksenstraße
Rochstraße
ALEXANDER-PLATZ
Rathausstraße
Spandauer Straße
Grunerstraße
Alexanderstraße
Magazinstraße
Voltairestraße
Littenstraße
Schillingstraße
Lichtenberger Straße
FRIEDRICHSTRASSE
Georgenstraße
Dorotheenstraße
Mittelstraße
Reichstagufer
Paul-Löbe-Allee
Platz der Republik
Reichstag
Scheidemann Str.
John-Foster-Dulles-Allee
TIERGARTEN
Tiergarten
Brandenburger Tor
Straße des 17 Juni
Entlastungs Str.
Ebertstraße
Wilhelmstraße
Behrenstr.
Behrenstraße
H.-Arendt-Straße
Unter den Linden
UNTER DEN LINDEN
Universitätsstr.
Charlottenstraße
Oberwallstraße
Am Zeughaus
MITTE
Schloßplatz
Werderscher Markt
Breite Straße
Mühlendamm
Gertraudenstraße
Spreeufer
Poststraße
KLOSTERSTRASSE
Stralauer Straße
JANNOWITZBRÜCKE
FRANZÖSISCHE STRASSE
Französische Straße
Jägerstraße
Taubenstraße
Mauerstraße
Glinkastraße
Gendarmen-markt
Mohrenstraße
Mohrenstr.
Kronenstraße
STADTMITTE
HAUSVOGTEI-PLATZ
Niederwallstraße
Kurstraße
SPITTELMARKT
MOHRENSTRASSE
Leipziger Straße
KREUZBERG
Approximate scale
1 kilometre
1/2 mile
Lennéstraße
Voßstraße
Bellevuestraße
Tiergartenstraße
Entlastungsstraße
Herbert-von-Karajan-Str.
Philharmonie
Scharoun Str.
Potsdamer Straße
Ludwig-Beck-Str.
Vox-str.
Alte Potsdamer Straße
Linkstraße
POTSDAMER PLATZ
Stresemannstraße
Stauffenbergstraße
Sigismundstraße
Hitzigallee
Neue National-galerie
Marlene-Dietrich-Platz
Staatsbibliothek
Rud.-v.-Gneist-Gasse
Gabriele-Tergit-Promenade
Reichpietschufer
Schöneberger Ufer
Schellingstr.
Köthener Straße
Bernburger Straße
Dessauer Straße
Am Karlsbad
MENDELSSOHN-BARTHOLDY-PARK
Mendelssohn-Bartholdy-Park
Hafenplatz
Lützowstraße
Schöneberger Str.

To wander through Mitte (middle) is to cross back and forth between periods of Berlin's history and to experience its tumultuous history, dynamic politics and modern revival. No other part of the city has borne so much of the brunt of Berlin's troubled and painful past. With its royal and grand-bourgeois avenues, such as Friedrichstraße and Unter den Linden, artists' quarters in and around the former Jewish areas, the showy Alexanderplatz and the Museumsinsel (p. 17), Mitte changes its face on almost every corner and shares borders with nearly all the inner-city neighbourhoods, as well as bridging the western and eastern quarters. The district houses the government, international corporate headquarters, opera and theatre houses, small artists' sweatshops and galleries, as well as residents from the former Communist era, who live in social housing complexes surrounding Alexanderplatz – the so-called Plattenbauten seen in the movie *Goodbye Lenin*.

Unter den Linden, the symbolic heart of Mitte, embodies a typically German romantic preference for combining education with culture. It would be hard to find another grand avenue in any other city where huge buildings – palaces, churches and museums – have been preserved for their original purpose and no concession has been made to cheap tourism. Cross Unter den Linden and stroll along Friedrichstraße southwards to discover the remodelled shopping district or northwards, along the Torstraße, to experience the transition to the more bohemian and still comparatively untouristy Prenzlauer Berg.

Around Hackescher Markt, Berliners, tourists, artists and businessmen all mingle together amid the 18th- and 19th-century surroundings. A special housing type in Berlin, the Hinterhöfe, allowed the development of many sites into pedestrian passages that now host creative and original stores and cafés. In the centre of Oranienburger Straße, the rebuilt Jewish Synagogue is a visual indicator of the revivification Jewish culture has begun to enjoy over the past decade.

A stark contrast to the lively cultural and historic palimpsest that is Mitte, gleaming Potsdamer Platz has been rehabilitated from its destruction during the Second World War. Once thriving under the democratic Weimar Republic and renowned for its sophisticated urban life and cafés, it has been transformed once again into one of the busiest places in the city. Architect superstars such as Renzo Piano, Vittorio Gregotti and Arata Isozaki have created brave new high-rise buildings that have come to epitomize the reunification of Germany and Berlin's status as the gateway to eastern Europe. Now a catalyst for surrounding areas, the metaphor of Potsdamer Platz is clear: decaying quarters forgotten for too long are again beating at the heart of the city.

TELEVISION TOWER

1 Berliner Fernsehturm

Alexanderplatz

Many world cities boast modern telecommunication or observation towers, but Berlin's was an early feature of its skyline. During the Communist period, political leader Walter Ulbricht saw the need to build a powerful transmitter in the centre of East Berlin whose 368-metre (1,200-feet) height would be visible from across West Berlin. Intended as a potent architectural and political symbol, it was completed in October 1969 after more than four years of labour. Since reunification it has become a popular sign of the city and is still used for technical purposes. An interior renovation in the mid-1990s restored its sky-top restaurant and its huge spherical chandelier, both a dramatic backdrop to a revolving restaurant and bar on the indoor observation deck.

AN ISLAND OF CULTURE

2 Museumsinsel

River Spree

A unique homage to history, art and the achievements of mankind is located on an island aptly called 'Museum Island' on Berlin's River Spree. In a space officially donated to 'art and science' by Friedrich Wilhelm IV, five impressive museums were built between 1824 and 1930, and in 1999 they were together designated a UNESCO World Heritage site. The museum ensemble was completed by what has arguably become the world's most famous collection of ancient historical artefacts: the Pergamonmuseum is named after the 16-metre- (52-foot-) high Pergamon Altar of Zeus that dates back to a 164 BC royal temple in Bergama, Turkey. The Museumsinsel suffered extensive damage during the bombing of Berlin and subsequent neglect during the period of the city's divide, but a massive restoration project led by British architect David Chipperfield will continue until 2020, by which time all the museums will be connected by subterranean walkways. The quintet consists of the Neues Museum (New Museum for the history of humanity, due to re-open in 2007), the Alte Nationalgalerie (Old National Gallery), the Altes Museum (Old Museum, now restored after suffering bomb damage in 1943 and home to ancient art and sculpture), Bodemuseum (displays of medieval coins, sculpture and art, re-opened in 2005) and the Pergamonmuseum. All the museums are overlooked by Berlin's Protestant cathedral, the Berliner Dom. Completed in 1905, it is open to the public and if you can climb the few hundred stairs, it is worth the trek to the upper balcony that wraps around the dome and provides a bird's-eye view of the island and city beyond. For a fish-eye view, one of the district's most unusual attractions has recently opened within the DomAqurée office block opposite the Berliner Dom: in the central atrium is AquaDom, a huge, 14-metre- (46-foot-) high column-shaped aquarium that features a lift running up its centre, ideal for culturally burnt-out visitors to cool down surrounded by moon- and angelfish.

HISTORY IN THE MAKING

3 Deutsches Historisches Museum

Unter den Linden 2

'Enlightenment and communication' with a view to 'striving to help the citizens of our country gain a clear idea of who they are as Germans and Europeans, as inhabitants of a region and members of a worldwide civilization' is the official mandate of a museum whose definition has changed since 28 May 1695, when the Elector Friedrich III of Brandenburg (who after 1701 called himself King Friedrich I of Prussia), gave the orders to lay the foundation stone of the Berlin Zeughaus. What started as the German arsenal collection became the German Historical Museum in 1990, when the West German Deutsches Historisches Museum, which was established in 1987 but had not yet found a home, took over the building and contents of the Zeughaus and the East German Museum of German History, its previous inhabitants. Most recently, the building, which was restored by Friedrich Schinkel after 1815, assumed a more contemporary architectural character. I. M. Pei, famous for his glass pyramid at Paris's Louvre, was invited to work his shape-changing magic on the museum. His light, glass and marble structure created a further 2,700 square metres (29,000 square feet) of space for temporary exhibitions when it opened in 2003. This is in addition to the large Zeughaus where Germany's tumultuous history from the 9th century to the present is set out as a permanent exhibition.

DRINK UP

4 Bar

Karl-Marx-Allee 36

Bar's huge glass façade is a living window display of fine liquors. The box-like space casts a view down the equally grand scale of the Karl-Marx-Allee in all its processional splendour. The interior design makes the dramatic architecture the focus, so that, apart from a gaggle of screaming socialites after 10 p.m., there is very little inside. All the mayhem can be observed from a slightly more tranquil second level.

CUTTING EDGE

5 WMF

Karl-Marx-Allee / Schillingstraße

Their name is lifted from a cutlery-producing company (Württembergische Metallwaren Fabrik), the interior from the Palais de la République (formerly the heart of East Berlin). The boys at WMF metamorphosed themselves several times before arriving at their current state of being, an electronic dance music venue with three record labels and a radio station producing leading-edge electronic music. Sunday's Gay Tea Dance is a camp crowd-puller, but a perusal of the programme will yield music to suit all (adventurous) tastes almost every night of the week.

THEATRE OF THE PEOPLE

6 Volksbühne: Roter Salon and Grüner Salon

156

POETIC PUZZLE

7 Kaffee Burger

Torstraße 60

Spoken-word poetry jams have always been associated with Kaffee Burger, as one of the owners is poet Bert Papenfuss. Building on the reputation it gained for literary discussions during the Communist era, he re-opened the bar in 1999. His own underground influence is augmented by the Russian cultural commentator Wladimir Kaminer, who rose to cult fame with his Russian interpretations of Berlin and the best-selling book *Russian Disco*, and who occasionally DJs at the club. The venue is frequented by a crowd hungry for alternative entertainment, and they are rarely disappointed, as Papenfuss encourages readings, film screenings and live bands, always followed by a musical cross-section from local DJs.

APRÈS SKI

8 Nola's Am Weinberg

Veteranenstraße 9

This little piece of Switzerland in the heart of Berlin is Stefan Schneck's third restaurant in the city (his first, Nola, is in Tiergarten; the second, an Australian eatery called Woolloomooloo, is in Charlottenburg). Atop a sloping lawn in the Weinberg park and overlooking its greenery, this former dive disco was transformed into an über-modern chic ski shack, with warm natural wood on the walls, floor, tables and chairs. A huge terrace catches the sun from dawn till dusk, and with Schneck's stock of official Swiss military blankets guests are encouraged to catch the rays even in the winter. Fare includes Alpine favourites, such as cheese fondue and raclette, but in the summer lighter dishes dominate; all year round a vast, Swiss-style buffet breakfast is served all day.

SPOT THE ARTISTE

9 Maxwell

HONEYMOON HOTEL

10 Honigmond Garden Hotel

RETURN TO SENDER

11 RSVP Papier in Mitte

RECORDED VINYL

12 Digalittledeeper

Torstraße 102

As you walk by the front of Dagmar Maziejewski's shop Digalittledeeper, you will most likely encounter two people, earphones clamped to their heads, bent over decks, expressions of deep-mix concentration knitting their brows. Maziejewski achieves the perfect window decoration by fitting two Technics decks in an alcove facing the street, knowing it will lure DJs and their wannabe brethren. Maziejewski moved from Cologne in 2002 to run the vinyl depot selling a mixture of electronic, hip-hop and jazz alongside a wholesale mail-order business. 'Berlin's music scene is happening,' Maziejewski says. 'There is a second wave of music people moving here.'

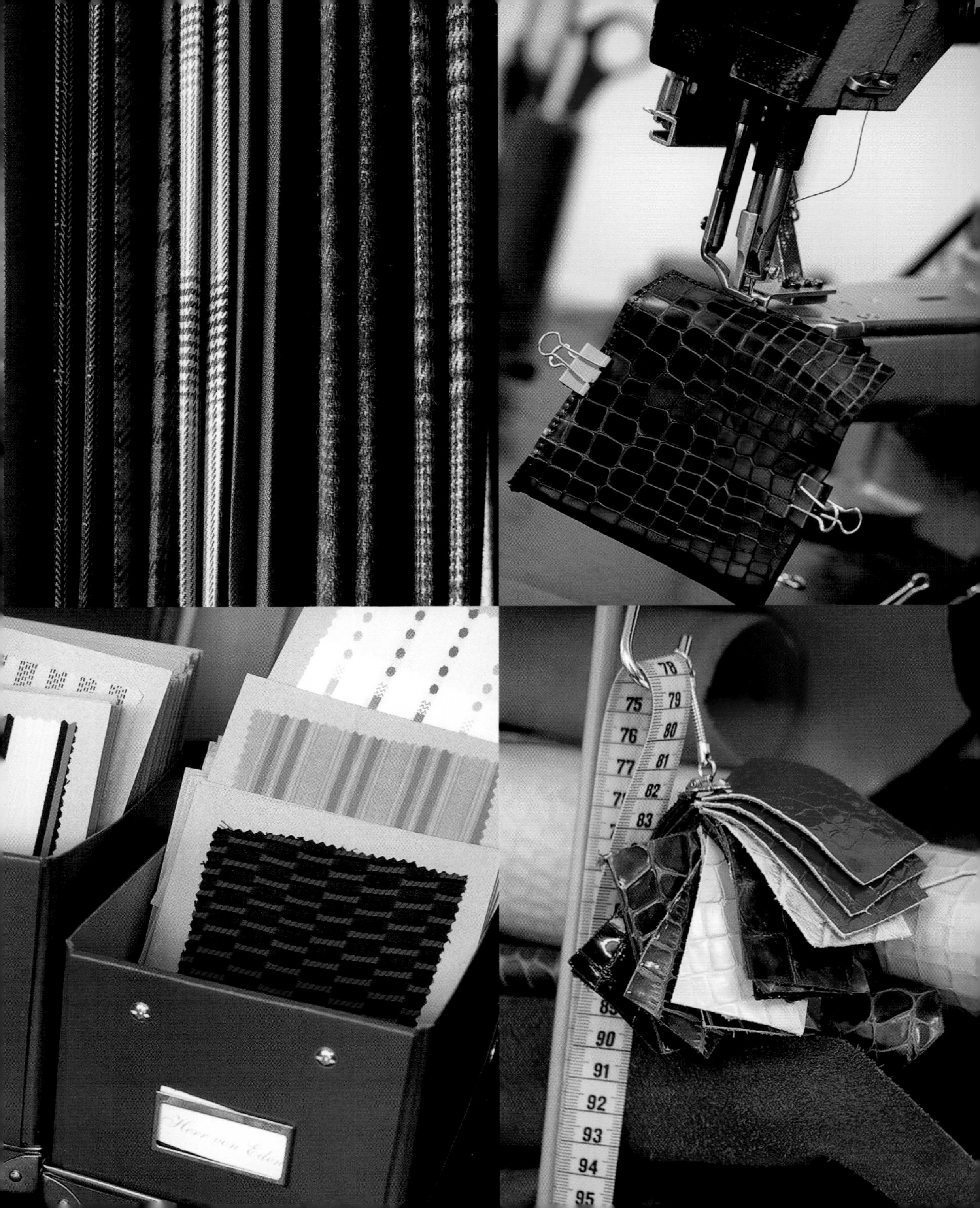

Herr von Eden
78
75
79
76
80
77
81
82
83
90
91
92
93
94
95

BITS AND BAGS

13 TaschenDesign Accessoires

Torstraße 97

Monia Herbst is one of Mitte's bright young designers, going it alone in a little shop that doubles as atelier and retail space. A native of Germany's Brandenburg region (of which Berlin is part), she studied fashion design in the city and by graduation was specializing in bags. 'My bag designs are very straight, strong and simple,' she comments. 'I like clean lines and always use very soft leather, so the resulting bag looks solid to the eye but is soft to the touch.' In 2003 Herbst opened the semi-subterranean workshop, and her use of contrasting colours and wild animal-printed leather in wallets, purses, key-ring holders and bags draws the eyes of passersby. One of her most publicized creations is the 'tuxedo for bottles': multifaceted holders (from mono- or multicoloured leather strips) that slip over the heads of bottles, forming fantastic protective covers for wine bottles or empty bottle vases.

SUITED AND BOOTED

14 Herr von Eden

Alte Schönhauser Straße 7

Often modelling his own work, natty dresser Bent Angelo Jensen mirrors his own slimline suits, hanging on one side of his men's clothing store, with classic vintage two-and-three-pieces on the other. Although rarely present in the store himself, he can be seen there as the man wryly posing on the posters that hang in the back room and in the pictures taken for a very nifty and collectable flip-book. Inspiration is drawn from vintage suits from the 1920s to the 1940s, and customers choose the fabric for their tailor-made shirts from boxes filled with vintage swatches: of the 300 samples there is only enough to make one shirt of each. The store design, also by Jensen, is another tribute to this era, with cotton shirt fabric hanging halfway down the wall and a smoky mirror border above cork tiles. The clothes are enhanced by a choice selection of vintage (but unworn) shoes and ties, hats and cufflinks.

FEEDING FRENZY

15 Kochlust

Alte Schönhauser Straße 36–37

Brit Lippold may have a nine-to-five job as a civil servant, but her true passion is food. A visit to London's Books for Cooks bookstore in Notting Hill inspired her to establish an equivalent in Berlin, and Kochlust means what it says: a passion for cooking. At the back of her self-designed shop is a huge kitchen where lessons are held and the results eaten at a dining table permanently laid for twelve. Most books are in English, but her penchant for French cuisine has put a few gourmet volumes on the shelves. More familiar to Germans are *Backbuch* and *Schulkochbuch* by Dr Oetker, who, though now in his seventies, has been teaching the nation to cook for more than 30 years. 'Steak topped with a fried egg and a side order of gherkins' rather dates him, but his sentiment, 'Backen macht Freude' – 'baking gives pleasure' – has never changed.

BLACK RAVEN, WHITE LINEN

16 Schwarzenraben

Neue Schönhauser Straße 13

The interior is deep, the façade impressive. The fact that the space was a cinema during the 1920s with separate screens for men and women goes some way to explaining the size of this restaurant. One leather banquette stretches 45 metres (150 feet) to the point where the restaurant opens into a garden, which is used for al fresco dining during the warmer months and which contains the eatery's eponymous raven sculpture. Serving mainly Italian fare, the locale is split into a café-brasserie offering simple soups and snacks that can be eaten at dark wooden tables or the bar, and a sand-toned restaurant with linen-covered tables lit by low, sensual lighting.

IN AND OUT

17 Breathe

THE SECRET ART GARDEN

18 Sammlung Hoffmann

Sophie-Gips-Höfe, Sophienstraße 21

A neon glow of hot red, nauseous yellow or icy blue is the visual siren that lures you off the street into this den of contemporary art. The unexpected installation situated between Sophienstraße and Gips Straße is the property of Erika and Rolf Hoffmann, who bought it after the Wall fell in 1989 to house their extensive art collection. Typifying the gentrification of the Scheunenviertel, they restored the courtyard and lined the entrance ceilings with neon lights, creating different mood areas. The Hoffmans also live here and open their art-filled home to the public for appointment-only tours on Saturday afternoons. This unconventional 'gallery' boasts a floor installation by Pipilotti Rist and pieces by Felix Gonzales-Torres, Nan Goldin and Douglas Gordon. Viewing in these intimate surroundings is a privilege.

LIVING MACHINE

19 Wohnmaschine

Tucholskystraße 35

In 1988 the old Jewish quarter of Mitte was not the desirable part of town it is today. Friedrich Loock was born and lived there, and threw an art party in his apartment with artist pal Robert Lippok. Nothing sold, but its success prompted him to host art projects, until his home became a permanent gallery space. He gave it the Le Corbusier–inspired name to avoid awkward questions from the Stasi, as the DDR regime discouraged galleries and people were unwilling to give their name to one. Only after the Wall came down did Loock attempt to run the place commercially, although he admits that 'I sold nothing for the first four years'. Since then, his home has become an epicentre of Berlin's cutting-edge art world. Loock looks after painter and sculptor Peter Rösel and nurtures Japanese talents in Europe. One of his protégés, Miwa Yanagi, recently showed at the Deutsche Guggenheim.

A LITTLE LINGERIE

20 Blush

Rosa-Luxemburg-Straße 22

Enter the flirtatious fantasy of Claudia Kleinert, who opened her purple salon in 2001 selling a selection of own and other labels that make up what can only be described as sophisticated undergarments for girls who want to have fun. Kleinert's contribution to the range comes in the form of lavender satin jumpsuits, silk caftans, velour dressing gowns and pastel morning jackets, as well as risqué sheer silk slips. Recently added to the Blush label are deliciously scented white or dark chocolate bars, which dissolve in bathwater. The centrepiece of the salon is a king-sized original bed from the 1970s (complete with a knob-tune radio built into the headboard), which has been re-upholstered in brown velvet and is used to display the panties, stockings and suspenders from Marizia by La Perla; Roberto Cavalli; the girly, exclusive Parisienne line Fifi Chachnil; and vests made in a wool-silk mix by Oscalito, who have been using this 'recipe' for over 70 years.

URBAN DIMENSION

21 Pro QM

GO LIGHTLY

22 Holly

Alte Schönhauser Straße 4

Named for the lady who used to breakfast at Tiffany's, Holly was opened in 2002 by Christian Breil and Claudia Winkler as a new shopping experience for Berliners. They introduced a glamorous boudoir lounge atmosphere in a space that sells the work of twelve designers, including that of Breil and Winkler. He designs a quirky menswear range under the label c.beau (his initials and a pun on the French 'c'est beau'), whose central inspiration that men's clothing lines should offer more than just jeans and sweaters results in short trousers in tweed or felt that fasten below the knee, and sailor-style knitwear. Winkler's womenswear is called 'Lis'. Both make their clothes in the atelier basement, which doubles as a showroom for her evening gowns and an impromptu bar area. 'Our work and that of those we sell must all subscribe to one ethic: individual but affordable,' explains Breil. Like Miss Golightly, the store has enigmatic charm, and it is filled with champagne and sparkling wit during the frequent readings and fashion presentations hosted there.

BOARD LIFE

23 VorOrt

Alte Schönhauser Straße 47

Carsten Kunst spent his previous life teaching snowboarding instructors how to snowboard. As a homage to that period of his life, he called his fashion store Superfly for two years before settling in 2003 on the name VorOrt, which means 'suburb'. With partner Jutta Kolinka he selects a functional mix of German and Italian labels, many of which bring together the best of sport and street edge-wear. Matador is a German board-wear clothes label for women and men featuring garments from stretchy tight-fitting jerseys to heavy, waterproof, fleece-lined jackets. They also sell puffball faux-fur hats by local Kreuzberg designer Anya Koeniger under her label König Walter. There are bags, and a group of former bike messengers are designing a Bagjack range, which is durable and easy to wear while pedalling.

ÜBER FASHION ICON

24 Claudia Skoda

PLAY PEN

25 Sophiensaele

Sophienstraße 18

The Sophiensaele is renowned across German-speaking countries for its productions of contemporary dance, music and theatre. Often the first port of call for young, controversial talent to test their wares on a live audience, the theatre is not frightened of being an experimental ground for artists who want to explore language and style. It came to life in the autumn of 1996 with a premiere by Sascha Waltz, now an internationally acclaimed choreographer, and since then has featured literally hundreds of shows. Performance art and concerts also appear on the Sophiensaele agenda. The performance remit is Europe-wide, and the stage is open to non-German artists also. As such the space is an integral platform during many of the city's festivals. 'Dance in August', theatre festivals and the International Literaturfestival Berlin all use the Sophiensaele in their venue line-up.

BM

PECULIAR ART

26 Eigen + Art

Auguststraße 26

Auguststraße is sometimes referred to as Mitte's Art Mile, and Eigen + Art sits right in the middle. The gallery is run by Gerd Harry Lybke, who started his art empire in his native Leipzig and extended it to Berlin in 1992, as well as creating temporary galleries as far afield as London, Paris, New York and Tokyo. He is committed to raising the profiles of former East German artists and has seen some achieve international status, such as Dresden-born sculptor Ricarda Roggan. Lybke also represents Carsten Nicolai and Neo Rausch and has exhibited work by 1996 Turner Prize winner Douglas Gordon and 1997 Turner Prize nominee Christine Borland.

TURNING JAPANESE

27 Yoshiharu Ito

Auguststraße 19

Yoshiharu Ito arrived in Berlin in 1987 from his native Tokyo and has become that rare thing, an Asian settler in Berlin. Most of Ito's early jobs were designing opera costumes, but his love of fashion eclipsed his musical background when he opened his own shop in 1999, where he continues to sew and show his clothes. He moved from women's to men's lines, but having such a small team, he more recently decided to drop the women's and now sells solely for men. With only six or seven pieces, each collection is tight and small. 'I try to make classic suits with a clever quirky difference that express my own culture clash: the Japanese interpretation of northern European fashion,' Ito explains. One unusual example is a heavy purple jacket and trousers that when washed will slowly turn blue as the mauve dye runs out.

HOT HATS

28 Hut Up

166

NADA NOUGHT

29 NIX

165

SWEET TREATS

30 BonBon Macherei

Heckmann Höfe, Oranienburger Straße 32

Lemon drops, mint jubes and sugarcane candy are the delectable items with which Katja Kolbe and Hjalmar Stecher lure customers into their sweet-selling cellar. At least 25 varieties of hard candy are made on the premises by the husband-and-wife team. The scent of warm, melted sugar permeates the air as you walk by their subterranean confectionery, and entry into the brightly lit space reveals the secrets of sweet-making. Stecher creates candy in front of customers, starting with heating the sugar and glucose mix at 150° Celsius. Ten kilos of thick toffee are then rolled under a shape-cutting rolling pin, and the sweets come out the other end. Orange and lemon, pineapple, strawberry and apple flavours contrast with an aniseed and fennel mix or with peppermint, extra-sour lime and even caramel with cream. Kolbe and Stecher's speciality is the Berliner Maiblätter: tiny bright-green leaf-shaped sweets.

CHILD'S PLAY

31 Viel Spiel

Große Hamburger Straße 28

Andreas Frischmuth and Antje Zülow have three children and were always on the look-out for child-friendly, eco-friendly wooden toys. 'We love traditional toys and often test the games out at home before putting them on sale,' says Frischmuth. As a carpenter, his experience qualifies him to understand and make quality children's products. Where possible they stock family-run manufacturers, such as Fagus and Selecta; there are also cars, games and furniture by HABA, coveted wooden figures (animals and people) from Ostheimer, and durable stone building blocks manufactured by Anka-Steine, a company with a 100-year history. They advise buyers always to look out for the 'Spiel Gut' sticker. 'In Germany it is the quality mark as far as toys are concerned.'

TURKISH GRILL

32 Hasir

Oranienburger Straße 4

So popular there are now six in Berlin, Hasir is a Turkish restaurant chain run by six brothers. Three live in their native Turkey and three are in Berlin, the eldest, Mehmet Aygün, assuming his natural role as head of operations. He moved from Turkey to Berlin in the late 1970s and opened the first Hasir in Kreuzberg (home to the city's largest Turkish population). The grill restaurant is known for its chicken, lamb and beef, as well as kuver bread baked on an open coal-fired stove. A lot of effort has gone into this, the latest Hasir: a well-dressed, dignified doorman greets customers, and staff are proud that everything on the premises is, like themselves, 'A to Z Turkish original'.

PRIME FASHION

33 Thatchers

Hackesche Höfe, Hof IV, Rosenthaler Straße

'We see clothes as a reflection of moods, and as such our designs are a method of personality enhancement,' says Thomas Mrozek, half of the Thatchers design duo. He and Ralf Hensellek have been making and selling clothes from their first shop in Prenzlauer Berg since 2001. They now have two outlets in Berlin and one in Paris. Aspects of their work are intrinsically Berlin: they start with a glamorous dress and add a sporty twist that renders its style functional and 'street', an attitude notable in a recent collection of bags, belts and necklaces crafted from zips. Quirky takes on everyday items are perhaps the common ingredient of the label – even the name fits this idea. 'Thatchers was a London-centric name for us and although we may not have liked the ex-British Prime Minister's politics, we did admire her discipline.'

TRIPPING THE LIGHT FANTASTIC

34 Trippen

161

SUNNY SIDE UP

35 Brille 54

Rosenthaler Straße 36, Rosenhöfe

Brille 54 has been selling spectacles to the nation for over twenty years and now boasts four shops in the capital. *Brille* simply means 'spectacles'; 54 is the street number of the first shop, still on Kurfürstendamm. Former employee Michael Ledermann bought the chain in 1987 with fellow employee and business partner Michelle Eichhorst, and they opened a fourth branch in the Hackesche Höfe in 2002. The slim, rectangular space is a product of architects Alexander Plajer and Werner Franz, whose work is familiar to the city in Mini Car and BMW showrooms, as well as the Universum Lounge (p. 103). Along with all the major brands, Brille 54 sells IC Berlin, a company of three design students who have been making frames since 1996.

WHO'S THAT GIRL?

36 Lisa D.

Hackesche Höfe, Hof 4, Rosenthaler Straße 40–41

There's more than meets the eye at Lisa D. Her name, for instance, is Elisabeth Prantner, and the label name is her nickname, Lisa, coupled with the initial of her maiden name. She came to own a fashion design boutique in the Hackesche Höfe by an unusual route. As a feminist art activist and partner of milliner Fiona Bennett (p. 162) between 1990 and 1995, with whom she produced shows, Prantner neither studied nor particularly followed couture, though she did make her own clothes. When she found that friends wanted her pieces, she employed a seamstress and went wholesale. Good tailoring enhances the female form and the hats, jackets, skirts and dresses are boldly cut and colourful. Prantner is still active at art festivals, consulting on performance shows and garments. The shop also sells a dressier line by Melinda Stokes, whose Stoxx label reflects her love of rare textiles.

CONTEMPORARY ART

37 Kunst-Werke Berlin

Auguststraße 69

1990. A former margarine factory. Four art enthusiasts, Klaus Biesenbach, Alexandra Binswager, Philipp von Doering and Alfonso Rutigliano, looking to originate a space for artistic explorations. The result: Kunst-Werke Berlin (KW). From the start interdisciplinary projects were a vital element in the gallery's programming, and the shows held here helped build the reputation of artistic director Biesenbach, who is also chief curator at New York's Museum of Modern Art offshoot space, PS1, with which KW has strong links. KW has developed into one of the most important spaces for contemporary art in the world, with over 2,000 square metres (21,500 square feet) of gallery space and an ongoing artist-in-residence programme, which sponsored Hedi Slimane (now head designer for Dior Homme) for two years while he produced his photo diary of Berlin. The inner courtyard also presents permanent work by Dan Graham; a reflective broken cube of steel and glass, which doubles as the Café Bravo; a functional slide tube by Carsten Höller; and Pedro Reyes's child-friendly *Copola*.

FASHION INITIATIVE

38 GB

Auguststraße 77–78

Guido Bednarz is a rare species now in Mitte: an East Berliner who stayed exactly where he was and continued doing what he had always done, despite the dramatic changes happening around him. 'I always made clothes here, so 1989 made no particular difference to me.' His professional design history began as a costume designer, and from 1987 to 1990 he worked mostly for television. Bednarz's scope encompasses three lines: a men's and women's range that he produces in only one or two sizes but will make to fit if requested, his couture range and a glamorous evening wear collection. Although his style is not experimental, his full-length frock coats, glittering gowns and formal suits have ensured a loyal following.

HARK BACK

39 Hackbarth's

Auguststraße 49a

One of the earliest bars to open in back-street Mitte, Jürg Breburda's little watering hole has been going strong since 1992. Breburda now also owns the more tourist-friendly Hackesche Höfe café but Hackbarth's, being off the beaten track, attracts a more local clientele. A steeply angled, V-shaped marble-topped bar with gold-plated edge is the focus. Gold is picked up on the walls as well, but their lower half is clad in deep-blue tiles. Stone floors, high stools and a few tables provide the background to the all-day breakfast selection and toasted sandwiches and baguettes. At night the bar becomes the domain of serious drinkers.

VIVA LAS VEGAS

40 Riva

Dircksenstraße, bogen 142

Under the arches near Hackescher Markt S-Bahn station is a bar whose sultriness obviously derives from a Latin influence, in this case the glitter dust sprinkled by Italian soccer star Luigi Riva, who gave his name to this glamorous drinking hole. The curves of the vaulted ceiling are continued into a bar that is practically in the round. Walls are covered in multicoloured squares, the yellow, orange, turquoise and blue offset by the musty green of the banquettes and fresh white of the countless bar stools. With a footballer as owner, Riva attracts a glitzy crowd of thirty-somethings and offers a divine selection of cocktails to meet the needs of its cashed-up, card-carrying clientele.

ROSES ARE RED

41 Cara Tonga

INVISIBLE BAR

42 Unsicht-Bar Berlin

Gormannstraße 14

Berlin may not yet be the gastronomy capital of the world, but it is certainly a contender for being one of the most experimental and inventive. The 'invisible bar' provides a metaphorical glimpse into the world of blind people by inviting diners to eat their meals in a state of pitch darkness. There are already two pitch-black bars in Berlin and one in Cologne and others are following suit in France and Switzerland. The first Unsicht-Bar was the idea of acoustic designer Axel Rudolph, who uses his work in an exploration of unlit areas and is cofinanced by the association 'Arbeit fur Blinde und Sehbehinterte', which has plans for theatre, literature and music evenings. Diners are led by blind waiters into the restaurant, where three or four courses are randomly ordered, served and eaten. Dining becomes a challenge and senses not usually called upon for this purpose become crucial. Guests have been known to panic, but equally you could lie down while you dine – no one would know.

TASTING HOUSE

43 Absinth-Depot Berlin

Weinmeisterstraße 4

Like cocaine, absinth was made illegal in Berlin in 1923. Unlike cocaine, it was legalized in 1998, so connoisseurs Andreas Scherff and Bernhard Flöder opened their shop and tasting parlour to celebrate the stuff. They stock some twenty varieties of the liquor, which is sourced from small family-run manufacturers in Spain and France, alongside their own 60% proof variety. Others include Philippe Lasala (50%), Versinthe Blanche and Emile de Pernod, and all can be sampled in the gold-papered tasting room. The owners' interest in the drink is cultural as well as commercial, so the shop also sells books about or by famous absinth drinkers: Oscar Wilde, Toulouse-Lautrec, Baudelaire and Van Gogh, to name a few. In 1901 Picasso drew *Woman Drinking Absinthe*, which features a lady with a bemused expression, known among drinkers as an 'absinth face'.

REAL DESIGN

44 Gallery / Shop

Neue Schönhauser Straße 19

What used to be a shop selling only popular international brand Authentic, best known for durable plastic accessories for the bathroom and kitchen, now stocks other strong German and international design. Shoppers at Bettina Gerber's store can find two-tone geometric crockery from Thuringen-based Kahla, sturdy pieces by Rosenthal, delightful cutlery produced by Auerhahn, which includes one for baby with *Mein Erster Löffel* (my first spoon) engraved on the silver handle. Chunky bars of chocolate by Sinnvolle Schokolade make a sweet addition to the shop: the wrappers for full-milk, bitter and raisin-and-nut are printed with such evocative words such as 'Lust' (desire), 'Glück' (luck) and 'Gnade' (mercy).

ALL DAY I DREAM ABOUT SPORT

45 adidas Originals Store

IS IT KOSHER?

46 Beth Café

Tucholskystraße 40

The area of Mitte that has as its focal point the shimmering golden dome of the New Synagogue has always been the spiritual heart of the city's Jewish population. After reconstruction of the synagogue, which was completed in May 1995, its entrance was officially signed 'Centrum Judaicum'. But Berlin's long history of welcoming Jews goes back much further than this. Although the city's past has shown it to have a reputation for opposition to (in turn) kings, Prussia and Hitler, it was the first municipality to invite some twenty Jewish families to become residents in the seventeenth century. Today the largest Jewish community in Europe has made Berlin its home, and Jewish institutions, galleries and outlets are once again opening in the streets surrounding the New Synagogue. One such is kosher restaurant Beth Café, which is run by the Adass Jisroel Community and offers fantastic wholesome traditional Jewish cuisine. Visitors should not be alarmed by the armed, uniformed German police guards that patrol outside all the city's Jewish buildings, an unfortunate necessity in the reality of modern politics. This should in no way put a dampener on those set on enjoying bagels, matzohs, blintzes, knishes, kishkes, borscht, challah and rugelach.

Absint
Fee

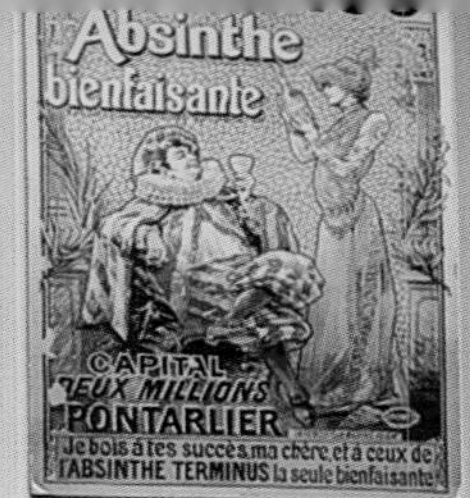
Absinthe
bienfaisante
CAPITAL
DEUX MILLIONS
PONTARLIER
Je bois à tes succès, ma chère, et à ceux de
l'ABSINTHE TERMINUS la seule bienfaisante
A
Absinth-Depot
Berlin

1. Absinth
DEPOT BERLIN
WEINMEISTERSTRASSE 4
10178 BERLIN
WWW.ERSTESABSINTHDEPOTBERLIN.DE
6,45 €

GODDESS GEAR

47 Penthesileia

Tucholskystraße 31

Drawing inspiration from the Amazon queen of Greek mythology, Sylvia Müller and Anke Runge joined forces in 1996 to make strong, feminine and shapely bags. 'We started with backpacks and changed their traditional form by moulding three-dimensional shapes that stuck out,' explains Runge, 'and we always put the zip on the inner bag, so our products are popular because they are so secure.' The collection has grown to encompass rare printed leather and dynamic geometric hand and shoulder bags. In 1999 Penthesileia added a dimension to the store by inviting in husband-and-wife jewelry designers Joachim Dombrowski and Marion Heilig, whose work appears under the label T31. Dombrowski concentrates on metal shapes, while Heilig uses novel materials such as phone cards to bring colour to her designs.

PLATFORM FOR LIGHT

48 Galerie Tagebau

Rosenthaler Straße 19

Galerie Tagebau is the collective brainchild of Michaela Binder (jewelry), Angela Klöck (hats), Ricky Schuchmann (fashion), Anke Schulz (ceramics) and Eva Sörensen (jewelry and vases), whose studio-cum-retail space opened in 1997 and is a respected platform for local designers. The designers occasionally change (and they feature guest pieces), but quality artistic work has been consistently associated with this space since DDR times. They all share the atelier and showroom space and take turns running and manning the store – but it is the work that is exceptional. Binder's metalworking skills manifest themselves in vessel bodies that protrude from copper and silver surfaces. She also uses acid-coloured felt or moodily dyed fur as the lining for gold or silver jewelry. Klöck's 'flying swan' hat was created from woven sisal and cockerel feathers and sits on the crown like a swan diving into water. Using textiles to explore shape and designing her own range of prints, Schuchmann's designs are functional and sculptural. Schulz's hand-turned ceramics are notable for their untreated exteriors and glazed insides, while Sörensen uses enamel to give colour and definition to her metal-based jewelry range.

IN REMEMBRANCE

49 Jewish Memorial

Große Hamburger Straße

Große Hamburger Straße is unofficially referred to as the 'Street of Tolerance', and it epitomizes Jewish culture in all its diversity. A Catholic hospital, a Jewish school and a Protestant church all share this street address. The most poignant historical reminder is a memorial at the south-eastern end of the street, on the site where a Jewish old folks' home once stood, but which the Gestapo turned into a deportation centre. Over 40,000 Jews were corralled here before embarking on their journeys to ghettos and concentration camps. The city's oldest Jewish cemetery was once behind this spot, but the only grave that remains is that of Moses Mendelssohn, the 18th-century philosopher who championed Jewish freedom and was forefather of the Berlin Mendelssohn dynasty that numbered composers and architects among its esteemed family members.

SMOKING AND DRINKING

50 Whisky & Cigars

168

MILLINER EXTRAORDINAIRE

51 Fiona Bennett

162

FUTURISTIC HISTORY

52 Re-Store

Auguststraße 3

The story of Re-Store began when Vaike Fuchs and Stefan Wecker met while working for a restoration furniture company in Berlin. Their love – for design and each other – led them to form their design agency in 2001, where they produce futuristic furniture and accessories. Their training as restorers has given Fuchs and Wecker an intimate understanding of the potential of materials and how they age or are prevented from corruption. From a conceptual starting point of re-use, they took lacquer sample plates from the automobile industry and turned them into a range of lounge furniture called Cubes. The duo have attracted extensive media praise, and their profile as a design agency devising 'flexible concepts for private and public interiors' is growing. They also have the endearing habit of wearing matching overalls.

DEMOLITION DERBY

53 Tacheles

Oranienburger Straße 54–56

Even in Berlin, in its constant construction flux, Tacheles is a shocking structure. You cannot help but be captivated by the dereliction of the 1908 shopping arcade, made even more intriguing by the fact that it has been in this state since it was bombed during the Second World War. There were plans to remove the eyesore, but squatters prevented this in 1990, and since then it has been occupied by artists' studios and impromptu party organizers. There are restaurants, bars and even a cinema at ground level. Some last, some don't, but Tacheles lives on. Plans to restore the building to its former glory – or at least give it a façade that is not pockmarked and crumbling – remain temporarily on hold, thanks to city-wide budgetary constraints.

THE ROAD IS LONG

54 Schiffbauerdamm

• Berliner Ensemble, Theater am Schiffbauerdamm

From the 1870s until the Second World War this street was the focal point of Berlin's urban life. Bertolt Brecht's own theatrical stamping ground, the Berliner Ensemble, is still here and flanks the northern side of the redevelopment of the more conservative quarter of Mitte. The many bars and restaurants along this stretch – mostly dives – are popular with politicians and journalists, many of whom arrived in the past decade from the former capital, Bonn, and whose new parliamentary and media offices are nearby.

THE ART OF EATING

55 Engelbrecht

139

ART STATION

56 Hamburger Bahnhof

Invalidenstraße 50–51

Like a lighthouse beacon, Dan Flavin's blue and green neon installation radiates from the façade of a former railway station, hinting at the transformation that the Hamburger Bahnhof has undergone to become The Hamburg Station Museum for the Present. It opened in its current guise in 1997 with a permanent collection including pieces by Andy Warhol, Joseph Beuys, Cy Twombly, Robert Rauschenberg, Sol LeWitt and Bruce Nauman, much of it part of the Erich Marx bequest, that gives the main ground-floor space something of a late-1970s gloss. This is counterbalanced by an evolving temporary programme on the upper levels, including recent shows of sculptor Ron Mueck and Indian photographer Dayanita Singh, as well as an Australian group show, 'The Down Side Up'. The Bahnhof consistently attracts high-calibre international curators and artists, making it Berlin's destination contemporary gallery.

WINE GUY

57 WeinGuy

128

ART HOUSE HOTEL

58 Luise: Hotel + Künstlerheim

110

KÖNIGLICHE PORZELLAN MANUFAKTUR

59 KPM

Unter den Linden 35

Given the royal seal of approval by Friedrich II in 1763, KPM bears a logo of a blue sceptre. The Prussian king was passionate about porcelain, which he dubbed 'white gold'. Today synonymous with classic quality porcelain, all KPM's services are hand-made, hand-painted and signed by the motif maker. Over the years names such as Johann Gottfried Schadow, Trude Petri and Enzo Mari have been inscribed on KPM crockery. For over 240 years they have developed design lines that are now recognizable in their own right: the Bauhaus's Urania, Enzo Mari's Berlin and the opulent classic Kurland, created in 1790 for Prince Peter von Kurland. KPM also make specially commissioned pieces for gourmet restaurants throughout Germany, all made at their factory in Charlottenburg. This is one of two shops in Berlin (the factory outlet is also in Charlottenburg).

SIMPLY ELEGANT

60 Malatesta

Charlottenstraße 59

This is the third and latest in the reputable stable of Piero de Vitis, a native of Tuscany who has been living in Berlin for over 30 years. His first two restaurants made him a serious player in the city's gastronomic circles, but de Vitis maintains a hands-on method of taking care of business, no doubt a crucial element of his success. De Vitis insists on fresh produce, simply prepared, and the result is ample portions of fresh pasta stuffed with lobster, delicate fish given light moisture by a drop of rare oil and lemon juice; desserts are similarly classical: chestnut puddings, sorbets and traditional panna cotta.

RESERVIERT
Milagro
ZAPATA

SINCE 1811

61 Lutter & Wegner

MY NAME IS HELMUT

62 Newton Bar

LIGHT AND SPACE

63 Dorint am Gendarmenmarkt

FOOD GLORIOUS FOOD

64 Aigner

Am Gendarmenmarkt, Charlottenstraße 50–52

The name of the restaurant at hotel Dorint am Gendarmenmarkt (p. 114) comes from the Viennese Café Aigner, founded in 1903 but closed in the 1980s. The original Jugendstil Thonet furniture was salvaged from the Austrian café, restored and now adorns the namesake restaurant in Berlin. With over 130 seats (some original) and a private billiard-club–dining room, eating at Aigner can be a social or an intimate affair. The restaurant has mirrors on the ceiling and black teak wooden tables, and room dividers that double as shelving cabinets create a restrained comfort. There are several menus: at least five three- to four-course business lunches, a Viennese selection, a German variation and Berlin and Brandenburg regional cartes as well. Duck holds pride of place in this kitchen and appears in some form or other on almost all of the menus.

OREO DIGESTIF

65 Cookies

Charlottenstraße 44

This club is the stuff of Berlin legend. 'Cookies' is the pseudonym of an enigmatic club entrepreneur whose own underground nights began as a techno DJ in the early 1990s. His own parties were private affairs and punters were only allowed through the door if they knew the password. This coveted information was spread first via word of mouth and later through text messaging. The Cookies venue is his first permanent club and is popular with the city's fierce young Turks (metaphorically and literally). He has recently added a restaurant, Cookies Cream to his after-hours emporium, housed in a defunct hotel building. Decadently derelict, the restaurant contrasts deconstructed walls (think loose wires and bare brickwork) as the backdrop to ironed white linen table-cloths under neatly set-out silverware. With dancing as dessert, the cuisine is appropriately light and predominantly vegetarian. Bookings should be made in advance.

MORE THAN A NICE CUP OF TEA

66 Tadschikische Teestube/Die Möwe

145

A PARLIAMENTARY AFFAIR

67 Dachgarten

HOTEL LORE

68 Hotel Adlon Kempinski

BETTER BEER GARDEN

69 Menardie

Alt Moabit 143–45

Located in the salubrious new developments of the Regierungsviertel (government quarter), in front of Chancellor Schröder's own office, Menardie is an upmarket beer garden. Hand-picked pebbles are scattered over the ground instead of sand, and its water-feature is the River Spree. There is continuing development in the area, so the attractions of Menardie are best enjoyed in the warmer months, as plans to open a winter garden are still on the drawing board. Thought has gone into the design and menu: German and Moroccan titbits replace the usual whopping Bratwurst and Kartoffel (potato) salat. In 2004 a full restaurant in the redesigned *fin-de-siècle* building will be opened along with an oriental club in the basement. All designed by Swedish architect and designer Björn Cunerdings, who now lives in Morocco. Definitely worth the detour.

FROM RECENT PAST TO DISTANT FUTURE

70 Sony Center and Sammlung DaimlerChrysler

Potsdamer Platz

Helmut Jahn is the man responsible for a design that in its own way has become a symbol of reunited Berlin. The rising 'circus tent top' sits over the Forum of the Sony Center, a rather soulless entertainment centre made up of a geometric mangle of glass and steel, a few restaurants, the Berlin Film Museum, and a cinema and IMAX complex. To walk through it is to experience briefly what it might be like to live in the world of Ridley Scott's *Bladerunner*, an exhilarating monument of changing and reflecting lights

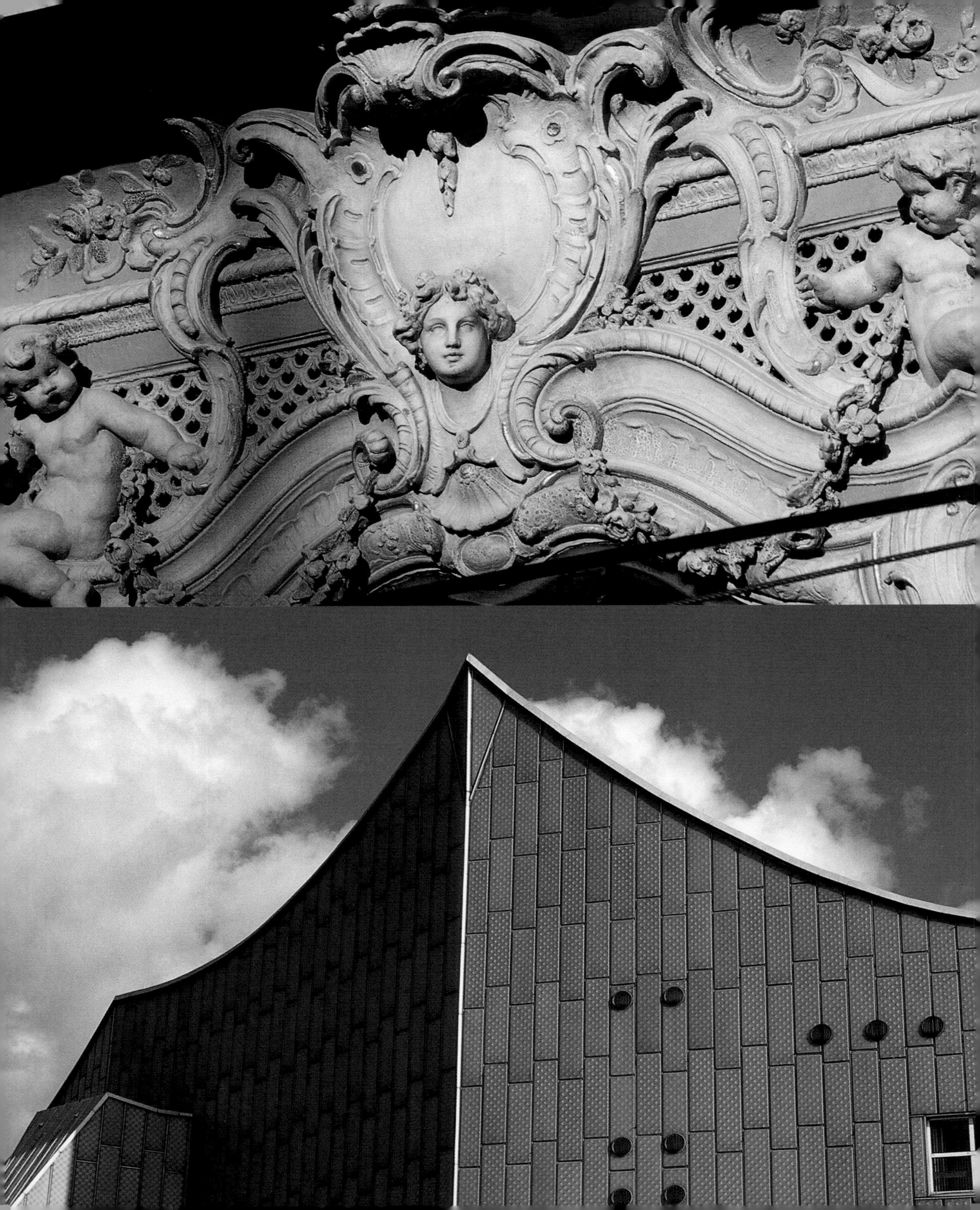

and moving elevators and escalators. Nearby DaimlerChrysler, which, like Sony, invested millions and has its own buildings on the Potsdamer Platz, has also opened a contemporary art space. The collection can be found in Haus Huth, the only remaining house on the Platz, and features four shows a year, including works by Andy Warhol, Jeff Koons and Josef Albers, among others.

BACK TO THE FUTURE

71 Kollhoff Building

Potsdamer Platz 1

The Sony Center is just one of the corporate residents of the reborn Potsdamer Platz. Another major player is DaimlerChrysler, which erected structures directly to the south of the Sony building. The car-manufacturing giants commissioned international architects, such as Renzo Piano, Richard Rogers and native Hans Kollhoff, who found inspiration in 1920s New York and designed a large, red-brick block whose angular corners bear comparison with New York's 1902 Flatiron building. Although many local architects ask what relevance that type of building has in modern-day Berlin, it is equally valid to ask where there is a single new building that has not received criticism. The Kollhoff isn't just a building to be appreciated from the ground: it has a public terrace from which you can see the new and controversial cutting-edge buildings that have sprouted up in central Berlin over the last decade.

URBAN SANCTUARY

72 Madison

116

CUE THE MUSIC

73 Qiu

157

BRIGHT YOUNG THING

74 Facil

140

THE EMPEROR'S CLOTHES

75 Kaisersaal

Bellevuestraße 1

In its pre–Second World War heyday, the Grand Hotel Esplanade was one of Berlin's social honeypots, but bombing destroyed 90 per cent of it, and what little remained was protected under German Landmark Preservation law after 1989. When the Sony Centre began construction in 1996, however, the Kaisersaal was in the way. Architects finally resolved the problem by moving the entire façade and original rooms some 75 metres (250 feet) from where they once stood. The inner walls have been reversed and, from behind protective glass, face outwards, with the result that passers-by can gain a glimpse of grandeur dating back to the era of Kaiser Wilhelm. The Kaisersaal (Emperor's Room), breakfast room and Silbersaal (Silver Room) are lavishly adorned in neo-Rococo and neo-Baroque style, and their situation today as part of Berlin's recent post-modern architectural fabric presents a certain comic irony.

MORE THAN MUSIC

76 Kulturforum

- Philharmonie, Potsdamer Straße 33
- Neue Nationalgalerie, Potsdamer Straße 50

Rising like a Saharan sand dune from the concrete forms nearby, the yellow folds of Berlin's Philharmonie need little introduction to the student or lover of 20th-century architecture. Designed and built in 1960–63 by Hans Scharoun to replace a complex of music halls destroyed during the Second World War, the venue for classical, modern, orchestral and chamber music is also the home of the Berlin Philharmonic Orchestra, currently in the energetic hands of Briton Simon Rattle. Scharoun placed seating 'in the round' – around the stage – a strategy recently used by Frank Gehry for his Disney Hall. To experience the acoustics and engineering is uplifting; to hear and see a performance sublime. The Kammermusiksaal (chamber music hall) by Edgar Wisniewski was completed only in 1987 but to specifications originally laid down by Scharoun. Although it contains a respectable collection of early German Expressionism, the main reason to visit the Neue Nationalgalerie, a steel-and-glass temple of Modernism, is to appreciate one of the last works of 20th-century master architect Mies van der Rohe, a founding father of the Bauhaus in Dresden and iconic skyscraper-builder in the USA. Designed from Chicago and built between 1965 and 1968, the building buries the permanent collection underground, providing an airy free-floating space at ground level for temporary exhibitions. A must-see for any follower of modern design masterpieces.

Prenzlauer Berg

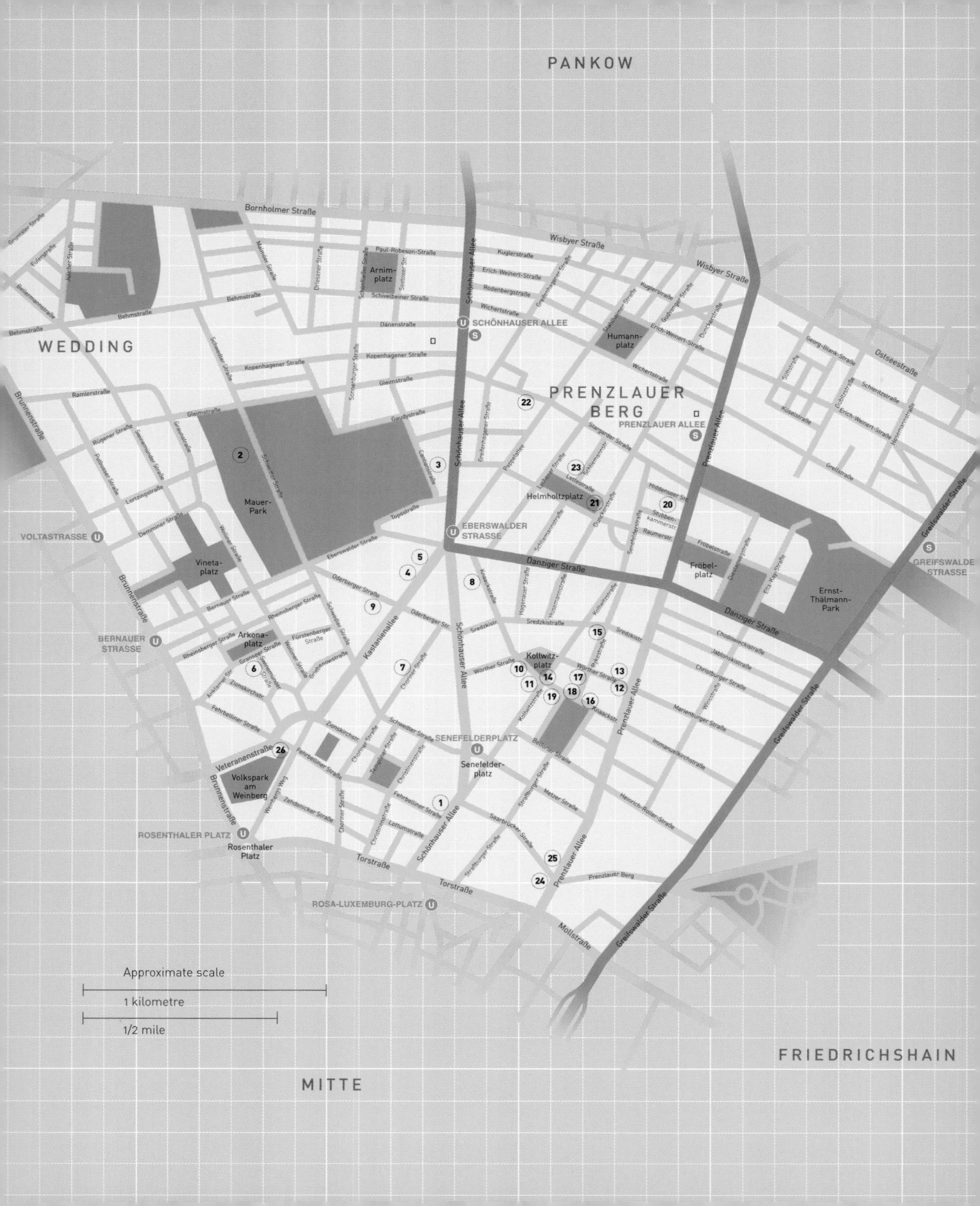

PANKOW

WEDDING

PRENZLAUER BERG

MITTE

FRIEDRICHSHAIN

Bornholmer Straße
Wisbyer Straße
Paul-Robeson-Straße
Kuglerstraße
Erich-Weinert-Straße
Rodenbergstraße
Wichertstraße
Schivelbeiner Straße
Behmstraße
Dänenstraße
Kopenhagener Straße
Gleimstraße
Ramlerstraße
Gaudystraße
Rügener Straße
Lortzingstraße
Demminer Straße
Topsstraße
Eberswalder Straße
Oderberger Straße
Bernauer Straße
Rheinsberger Straße
Fürstenberger Straße
Granseer Straße
Zionskirchstr.
Fehrbelliner Straße
Veteranenstraße
Zehdenicker Straße
Torstraße
Mollstraße
Danziger Straße
Sredzkistraße
Wörther Straße
Kastanienallee
Schönhauser Allee
Prenzlauer Allee
Greifswalder Straße
Ostseestraße
Georg-Blank-Straße
Schieritzstraße
Stargarder Straße
Lychener Straße
Raumerstr.
Fröbelstraße
Chodowieckistraße
Jablonskistraße
Christburger Straße
Marienburger Straße
Immanuelkirchstraße
Heinrich-Roller-Straße
Metzer Straße
Saarbrücker Straße
Straßburger Straße
Belforter Straße
Knaackstr.
Schwedter Straße
Choriner Straße
Templiner Straße
Christinenstraße
Lottumstraße
Brunnenstraße
Prenzlauer Berg

Arnimplatz
Humannplatz
Mauer-Park
Vinetaplatz
Arkonaplatz
Helmholtzplatz
Kollwitzplatz
Fröbelplatz
Ernst-Thälmann-Park
Senefelderplatz
Volkspark am Weinberg
Rosenthaler Platz

SCHÖNHAUSER ALLEE
PRENZLAUER ALLEE
EBERSWALDER STRASSE
VOLTASTRASSE
BERNAUER STRASSE
SENEFELDERPLATZ
ROSENTHALER PLATZ
ROSA-LUXEMBURG-PLATZ
GREIFSWALDER STRASSE

1 2 3 4 5 6 7 8 9 10 11 12 13 14 15 16 17 18 19 20 21 22 23 24 25 26

Approximate scale

1 kilometre

1/2 mile

Since 1989 Prenzlauer Berg has become the breeding ground for quirky, turbulent, young creative energy in Berlin. Designers, artists, actors, entrepreneurs and architects and the bars and restaurants they frequent make for a uniquely European *quartier* feeling, which seems is more diluted elsewhere in the city. The young (and young at heart) inhabitants know 'Prenzlberg' as a place not only for dwelling but also for exploring a variety of lifestyles that are assimilated into the existing building fabric – the parks, squares and dilapidated infrastructure that form the remnants of the defunct former East Berlin – and using it as a laboratory for very live experimentation.

Prenzlauer Berg began life in the *Gründerzeit* (the founding of the German Reich in 1871) as a residential district for the working class. Most of the area's buildings were thus constructed along similar lines, lending the district a pleasing architectural coherence. Largely spared from the bombs that destroyed so much of Berlin during the Second World War, many streets still exhibit the stark Prussian aesthetic of the turn-of-the-century buildings, a window into the past for modern observers. The area has always boasted a high concentration of artists and political activists, and was the focus of much liberal resistance mounted during the Third Reich; during the Communist era, the crush of buildings and dense population provided safe houses and anonymity.

The recent gentrification of the area has been successful in part because current redevelopment plans dictate that real-estate investment companies are only allowed to buy one or two buildings per block for renovation and investment purposes. This has ensured a socially lively and colourful mix where the affluent and the less affluent coexist harmoniously. Just as theatre sets are installed for different productions on the same day, so too Prenzlauer Berg rings the changes throughout the day. In the morning you can enjoy breakfast at one of the cafés surrounding Helmholtzplatz or at Wasserturmplatz. At lunchtime try one of the countless eateries that line the main avenues such as Kastanienallee, or delve into the side streets, where you will find an assortment of small, original and affordable outlets. At night Prenzlauer Berg is transformed into a thrilling and vibrant place in which even Berliners can hardly keep track of all the venues that pop up around the neighbourhood. On Kollwitzplatz you can experience artists enjoying the relatively cheap living circumstances next door to the current president of the German parliament, on Helmholtzplatz a famous actor enjoying a leisurely afternoon on one of the many benches with a local *Hausfrau* (housewife) and on Kastanienallee the hip crowd mingling with the old social set from a bygone era.

MULTIFUNCTIONAL: PAST & PRESENT

1 Pfefferberg

Fehrbelliner Straße 92

Pfefferberg has a long history. From afar it may seem to visitors that it dates back to Roman times, as its façade resembles an ancient ruin, but the first brick was laid in 1841 to the plans of architect Arthur Rohmer. It took shape very slowly and was not 'finished' until the late 19th century. Named after the man who commissioned it as a brewery, it has also housed tenants as varied as Hoffmann-Schokolade and the Germania Brotfabrik (bakery). The 13, 500 square metres (145,300 square feet) were used as a forced labour site and air raid shelter during the Second World War and in DDR times as a bus parking depot. 1990 saw it open up to culture and Pfefferberg is currently in the hands of a trust that is renovating it. The international Akira Ikeda Gallery threw their inauguration show there for acclaimed artist Frank Stella and rumour has it that Vitra Design Museum will be moving in sometime during 2006.

ANOTHER BRICK IN THE WALL

2 Mauerpark

Between Eberswalder Straße and Gleimstraße

Meaning 'Wall Park' and occupying a long, slim rectangular area on the western side of one of the few remaining stretches of the Berlin Wall, Mauerpark is the green escape for Prenzlauer Berg. The park's main path is not much more than a dirt track frequented by walkers with very large dogs, but the Wall itself sits atop a steep bank with benches at its base, affording views over industrial Berlin's housing blocks, some overshadowed by the optimistic floating bauble that is the Fernsehturm (p. 17). During winter the park is barren, a stark backdrop from which to contemplate the culture once created by the city-divider, but in the summer the park becomes an impromptu 'bring-your-own' beer garden.

BREAKING FAST

3 Cantian

Cantianstraße 11

Set within an award-winning building designed by Michael A. Peter, the west-facing glass façade of brothers Ivan and Niko Gosevski's café-restaurant lets light and warmth flood into the space. The building itself is home to many of Prenzlauer Berg's hip young things, its vertically stacked cube apartments boasting phenomenal views over the adjacent Friedrich-Ludwig-Jahn-Sportpark. But the Gosevskis's café also holds an award: second prize for best breakfast in Berlin. For less than 15 euros two people can feast on salmon, cheese, turkey, fresh fruit salad, an assortment of breads and jams and a choice of orange juice, prosecco or coffee. They named their café after the street that honours Berlin architect Johann Gottlieb Cantian. Architect Peter has also 'kept it in the family': his sister Nico is responsible for the paintings and photographic prints that seal Cantian's playful, child-friendly, warm atmosphere.

BOYS IN THE 'HOOD

4 Eisdieler

Kastanienallee 12

Five guys and a lot of ideas have given Eisdieler's urban street gear a reputation unsurpassed by other Berlin design talent. Martin Ruffert designs under the labels Quid Pro Quo (quality board-sport wear) and Bowler, and Stefan Dietzelt creates DC (Director's Cut, a line of men's suits) and Presque Fini (French for 'almost ready', his women's range of chic jersey dresses and fur-lined muffs with pockets). Together they run the 'mother' label Eisdieler, which also features the work of Olaf Grützner (Wild Spirit, re-formed second-hand clothing), Ove Jepsen (Gossip 67, understated street wear with a clever twist) and Till M. Fuhrmann, whose TMF line features aggressively masculine necklaces and bracelets that resemble sharks' teeth but are actually sculpted bone and mahogany. Four of the five met at Lette Verein, a private design institute in what was old West Berlin; Ruffert's background is as a consultant for internationally well-known sports labels. The name Eisdieler connotes selling and dealing, while referring to the former ice-cream (*Eis*) parlour that was their first shop in 1995.

IN A CITY GARDEN

5 Pratergarten & Hecht Club

147

Eisdieler
Alice clar?
Ich kann
nicht
spray
Eisdieler
Eisdieler

BERLIN
www.potipoti.com

FURNITURE HUNTERS

6 RoomSafari

Swinemünder Straße 6

Product designers Christine Nogtev and Chu Chong founded their agency in 2001 with a mission to create 'products for relaxed living' and a name intended to evoke adventure. Their creative output includes office and store interiors, such as Breathe (p. 163), but the space at RoomSafari shows their unusual products and witty gadgets that give pause for thought and frequently laughter: each of six drinking glasses is identifiable by the number of rings engraved on it (one to six) so that users can always distinguish their own; a square blackboard, with chalk supplied, is hung from a coat hanger. RoomSafari's originality derives from an ability to transform everyday objects into unexpectedly useful items: a coat rack is five pieces of aluminium and wood built to lean on any wall.

BUILDING PLATFORM

7 suitcasearchitecture

Choriner Straße 54

Beate Engelhorn and Kristien Ring founded their studio in July 2001 as a 'forum for newcomers and innovative established architects to increase public awareness in the building culture' and 'a plea for our profession'. Ring was born in the United States, Beate in Germany, and the two architects met while teaching architectural design at the Technical University of Cottbus. Their work with students highlighted the fact that fresh talent struggles for public exposure yet it is the group that needs it most. 'The goal of our exhibitions is to show the development of an idea from start to finish. We are intrigued by the testing, evaluating, discarding and reworking that comprises the ingenuity in the work of designers and architects.' To this end suitcasearchitecture organizes exhibitions and competitions, such as the Lebkuchenhaus for Christmas for the best house made of chocolate and cookies, and produces catalogues of the shows.

BEER AND CULTURE

8 Kulturbrauerei

Schönhauser Allee 36–39

A great example of the appropriation and reuse of a derelict inner urban space, the Kulturbrauerei is housed in a mid-19th-century red-brick former brewery. In the early 20th century, the site was the main brewery for Berlin's well-known Schultheiss beer, but today the warehouses are home to a cinema complex, supermarket and vast music shop, Sound & Drumland. The trendy Soda bar and restaurant (whose menu notoriously offers insects) lie adjacent to an enormous beer garden. Culture comes courtesy of the dynamic young media companies who rent office space here and the Sammlung Industrielle Gestaltung (Museum of Industrial Design), whose shop sells the latest life-enhancing products.

BUNNY GIRL

9 Hasipop

Oderberger Straße 39

'The name ["bunny pop"] is nonsense,' says Claudia Fauth of her fashion label, 'but we liked it because we like bunnies and we like pop culture.' Fauth met design partner Esther Jacobi in 1999, and they began making clothes for themselves, 'just for fun, but people approached us and asked where we had bought them, so we created a line that we sold through a shop.' Once out of school they decided to take running the business into their own hands, and opened up their space to other local labels. Anne Schmuhl's trousers and jackets, Anja Lafin's shirts, 667's baby line and Lucid 21's girlie skirts and T-shirts sit well with the Hasipop ethos, which appears not to take fashion – or life – too seriously. Best-selling products include the 'hasi-string' (bunny-thong) and 'hasi höschen' (bunny-girl slip).

BEACH AND BATH

10 Strandbad

Wörther Straße 12

An ingenious combination of products for beach and bathtub was the idea of Marina Vassmer and Sylvia Rottenburger. 'Germany is so geared up to selling kitchens that we wanted to focus on that other room in the house where you spend so much time,' explains Vassmer. 'We also appeal to all seasons. In the winter people like to wrap up in pyjamas and robes and spend time at the sauna, and in the summer beachwear prevails'. Strandbad is an Aladdin's cave of delectable bath products, from Acca Kappa, an old Italian family who make brushes and soaps using only pure oils, and the local Berlin line '1000 & 1 Seife' by Xenia Trost, whose background as a graphic designer is apparent in her soap's quirky labels and fun fonts. Among the most popular items are cosmetic bags of traditionally made chenille by the classic German textile factory Seiler – customers are so taken by them that they use them as handbags.

ALSATIAN CUISINE

11 Gugelhof

Knaackstraße 37

'Yes. Bill Clinton ate here,' is the immediate response from staff to virtually any question not about the menu. Hans Nübel and Detlef Obermüller's restaurant is renowned for its exquisite Alsatian cuisine but will never escape from the story that on a visit to Berlin, President Bill Clinton happened to be driving by, saw the restaurant and insisted on eating there. The Alsatian region is a 'culinary oasis between the Rivers Rhine, Moselle and Saar, which flourishes because the locals like to eat well', according to Gugelhof. The name derives from Gugelhupf (typical German cakes baked in a round tin with a hole in the middle) and *Gasthof* (a rural guesthouse). Featured dishes include the one that Clinton ate, Choucroute Gugelhof, which combines sauerkraut, blood-sausage, pork belly and pork neck served with potatoes and mustard, and Tarte Flambée Alsacienne.

WINE AND DELI

12 Weinhandlung Baumgart & Braun

Wörther Straße 21

Marcus Baumgart opened the wine shop he designed himself in 1992 and, encouraged by his success, opened a second store in Mitte in 2002, where he stocks wines from all over the world. A central feature of the space is an original working stove covered in aquamarine tiles, which creates an inviting warmth in winter and acts as a soothing cooler during warmer months. Tradition is openly respected, the wine being displayed on huge metal shelves or presented in the wooden crates in which they were delivered. There is a large selection of German wines, with the Dr Loosen Riesling being the most famous (and pricey). Baumgart also sells a selection of perfect edible accompaniments to the drinks: olives, anchovies and capers from Spain, Italian infused oils and biscuits and locally baked bread.

CHARI-THAI

13 Mao Thai

Wörther Straße 30

Norbert Frankenstein was teaching in Japan when he made his first visit to Thailand and fell in love with the country and the cuisine. He grew particularly fond of the food in the northeast region of the country and made it his mission to import these dishes back to Germany, eventually opening two Mao Thai restaurants in Berlin (and one in Ireland). Perhaps it is unusual for a German to have opened Asian restaurants, but there is a genuine mission behind Frankenstein's approach: he staffs his places mostly with Thais whom he brings over and pays regular European wages that are worth a lot more to them when they return home after their 'catering tour of duty'. He also sends a percentage of the profits from the restaurants to Thailand to support local farmers and to give Thai youngsters a chance of a better education.

HISTORY REPEATING ITSELF

14 Kollwitzplatz

Kollwitzstraße, Knaackstraße & Wörther Straße

The Käthe-Kollwitz-Museum in Charlottenburg (p. 93) is testimony to the prolific talent of this artist, but Kollwitz lived at Kollwitzstraße 25 (formerly Weißenburgerstraße) in Prenzlauer Berg for 50 years, and the square that also bears her name contains a statue of her. This vibrant area, brimming with bars and cafés, is ripe with history, and the unmistakable Wasserturm (water tower), which brought Berliners their first taste of running water following its completion by British architect Henry Gill in 1875, stands imposingly south-east of the square. It stopped being used as a water tower in 1952, and has since then had several incarnations; the special acoustics have inspired the artist group Kryptonale to organize festivals with space-related sound installations in the subterranean 'cave' (Wasserspeicher) that was used to store excess water, and there are plans to turn the Wasserturm into apartments.

NOT JUST JEWELS

15 Tosh

Sredzkistraße 56

Established in 1993 (this flagship store opened in 2001), Tosh is a jewelry company that makes pieces that are vivacious, colourful and worn by women who like to be noticed. Thomas Schwender has achieved success at the wholesale level and through TV celebrities, who have made it a well-known brand in Berlin; some pieces have even made it to New York's Museum of Modern Art store. Schwender produces two collections a year: 'Every season I try to do something new. I think that is why Tosh has stayed popular, as I reflect what inspires me at any given moment.' He delights in surprising his clients and refuses to replicate a line even if it is commercially successful. 'The latest switch for me is that after ten years of Swarovski rhinestones, I have started to adapt to the versatility of plexi-beads, although I always come back to leather.' Delicate wrist chokers woven in brown, yellow, white and cream are testament to his artistic interpretations.

VISIONARY FASHION

16 Schelpmeier

Knaackstraße 20a

An unassuming space – bare wooden floor with light from a chandelier casting shadows on cornices – is where Gabriele Schelpmeier sells a mix of German and Scandinavian fashion. The modern yet classic décor is a reflection of the clothes: a mature but edgy selection from Danish NOA NOA, lingerie from DAY, as well as desirable lingerie and undergarments from German company Falke and quirky children's garments produced by her friend Claudia Benditz, which range from blue cords with red pocket piping to shimmering Chinese quilted jackets in gold and green. Schelpmeier herself produces pieces under the name Lorelay.

FINNISH HEALTH

17 Saunabad

Rykestraße 10

It is hard to believe that this sauna is in the heart of the city. With an inner court open to the elements, rock-covered floor, extensive foliage and eerie, spiritual wooden sculptures, Saunabad evokes an otherworldly air. From noon to midnight daily there is a choice of three saunas, freezing plunge-pool, reading sanctuary with reclining chairs, a garden and massages. To reach the piping-hot Finnish sauna, visitors walk across the garden (bring your own towel) to be bathed in natural light pouring through glass windows. A staff member hands out ice-cubes every hour before adding herb-infused water to the coals. Anyone who can't stand the heat at this point usually flops, pink, limp and panting, into the garden. The sauna is for both genders, except on Tuesdays, when it is reserved for women only.

DR ZHIVAGO

18 Pasternak

150

FASHION AND GALLERY

19 Sabine Kniesche

Knaackstraße 33

Sabine Kniesche loved art and clothes, but had a professional background in business; Sylvia Heise needed exposure in Berlin. And so began a mutually gratifying partnership over a decade ago; their shop moved to this location in 2002 but had always been local. Heise is a former East Berlin fashion student whose style is mature but with a sexy twist. Long-sleeved dresses are fastened only with poppers, tactile angora sweaters are patterned with subtle crosses and a skirt resembling wet rocks is made from polyester interwoven with metallic thread, enabling it to mould to the wearer's shape. Wall space is used to promote artists, and every month there is a new show.

LATIN LANGUAGE

20 Mutabilis

Stubbenkammerstraße 4

'The name is the fashion,' proclaim Silke Jentsch, Franziska Erler and Annett Oeding, the three women who make up Mutabilis, the label of feminine, fitted, confident clothing designed for 'the modern woman' since 2001. The Latin name of their shop can be translated as 'changeable' or 'multifaceted'. With this in mind, the trio produces three separate lines, distinguished as 'trend', 'young classics' and 'evening fashion'. All their pieces demonstrate the girls' ability to tailor innovative clothes from sexy fabrics. Stretchy faux-leather corsets hug the waist, the bust is swathed in smart bleached white cotton, monocle chains are added to pin-striped suits and below-the-knee skirts in layers of sheer chiffon swirl to give an occasional glimpse of thigh.

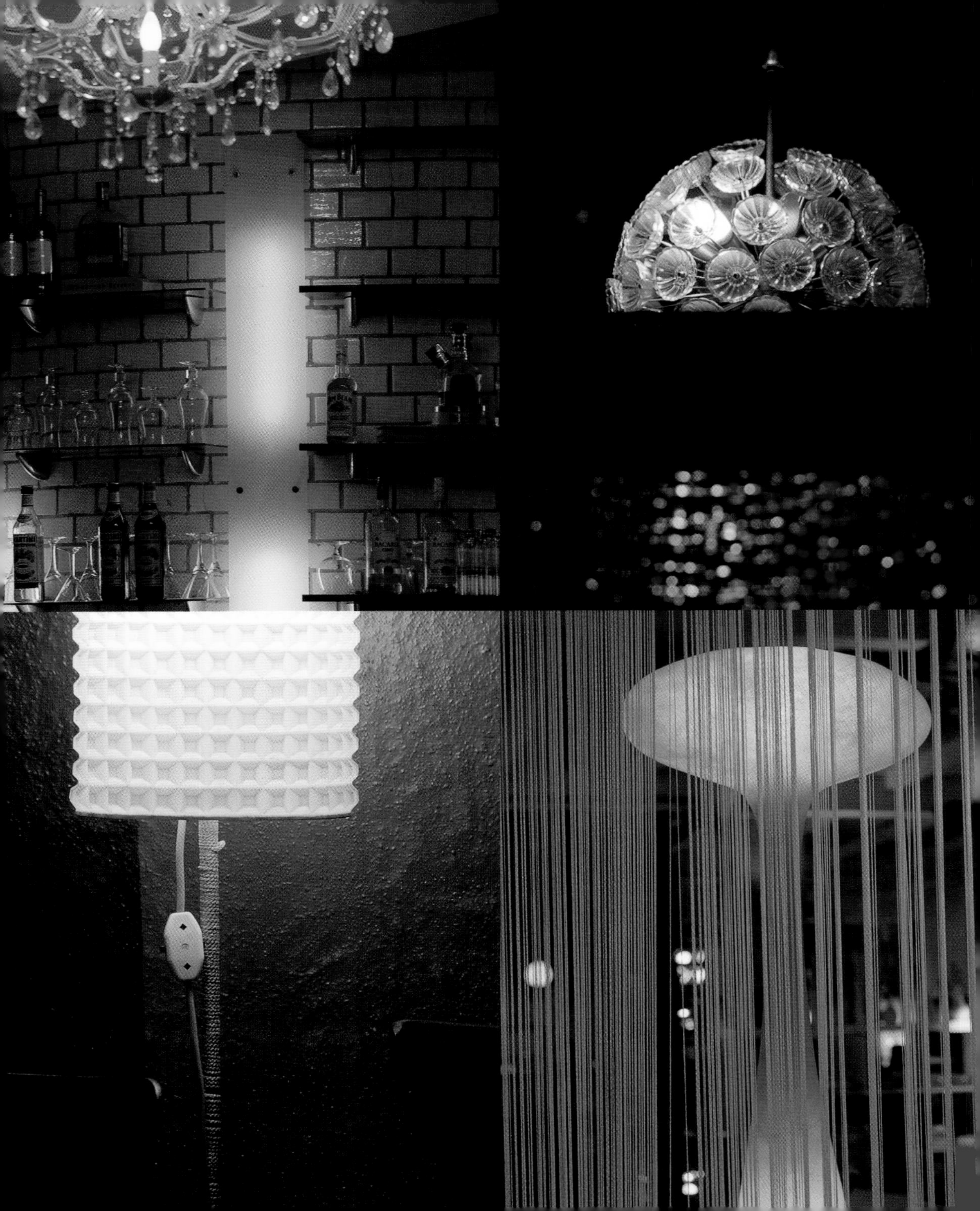

CHOCOLATE ADDICT

21 In't Veld Schokoladen

171

WHO'S THAT GIRL?

22 Marietta

Stargarder Straße 13

Torsten Behrend's little café exudes a warm, golden hue. The space has a front and back room, and each is an expression of Behrend's love and knowledge gleaned from his previous career as a dealer of period furniture. He has filled the lighter front room with chairs, tables, lamps and the odd magazine rack, all original pieces from the 1950s. By contrast, low sofas and side-tables from the 1960s furnish the darker back room, 'the cocktail area'. Behrend scoured antique fairs to find his unique selection, which of course is only the backdrop for a menu of breakfasts, soups, cocktails and the typical former East Berlin dish *Schwedeneisbecher* (Swedish ice-cream coupe).

LIVING ROOM WITH BREAKFAST

23 Wohnzimmer

Lettestraße 6

The name 'Living Room' reflects the relaxed atmosphere here rather than the décor. Anyone whose living room actually looks like this is either a true bohemian with hygiene issues or someone needing to see the 'house doctor'. It is quirky, with stripped walls left bare, grouting exposed around parts of tiles surrounding a random sink in one of its four rooms, and no two pieces of furniture match. Reindol Klenner opened Wohnzimmer as a bar in 1998, which has since expanded because the unorthodox ad-hoc approach proved popular (the fourth room was acquired by knocking down a wall in 2002). Wohnzimmer attracts local characters and is rarely empty, even on weekdays (partly, perhaps, because of the disproportionate number of self-employed designer residents in the area). The menu is simple: essentially, breakfast and cake.

FURNITURE EMPORIUM

24 Exil Wohnmagazin

Backfabrik, Prenzlauer Allee 250

Twelve hundred square metres (13,000 square feet) of open, concrete-walled space filled with a choice selection of contemporary German and Italian furniture and accessories will make interiors-lovers go weak at the knees. Opened in 2003 in a former bakery, Backfabrik, this is the second outlet for Peter Detlefsen, Micka Hillmeb, Sunito Karthaus and Conny Neiber (their first came into being in Kreuzberg in 1998 and occupies a similar area, imaginatively laid out in 21 rooms over four floors). The Prenzlauer Allee shop is a huge open room and celebrates loft living. The pieces – by Berlin designers Hausfreund and German ICE Dealer, among many others – are scouted by the owners, who promote the stores as platforms for new international design rather than merely furniture shops.

NIGHT DREAMER

25 Nocti Vagus

Saarbrücker Straße 36-38

It is no longer the only one, but Nocti Vagus does lay claim to being Berlin's first dark restaurant. Enter the world of Berlin engineer Simone Glosch, who built an underground dining room in which customers must eat in complete darkness, to heighten the use of the non-visual senses. Frustrated by distracting street noise, she wanted to create a pure listening environment in which sound could be savoured. A meal is served in complete darkness while live events – jazz or classical music, 'dark readings' or 'experience evenings' – programmed by Antje Schulz fill the air. Several people have opted to come here on 'blind dates', proposed marriage or even exchanged wedding vows in a room where they cannot see their partner's face. An interesting role reversal is part of the experience for sighted guests: they must relinquish control and form intimate tactile relationships with one of the seven blind waiters who run the space and who becomes a trusted link for them. The menu is set, but requests are taken, unless you want to give up your options and choose the 'Sensory Surprise'.

WINERY

26 Weinerei

168

Partyservice
MULINO BIANCO
Ritornelli
Abbracci
Pan di Stelle
Tenerezze
MILANO
Bianco
2,49
SAPORI

Kreuzberg
Friedrichshain

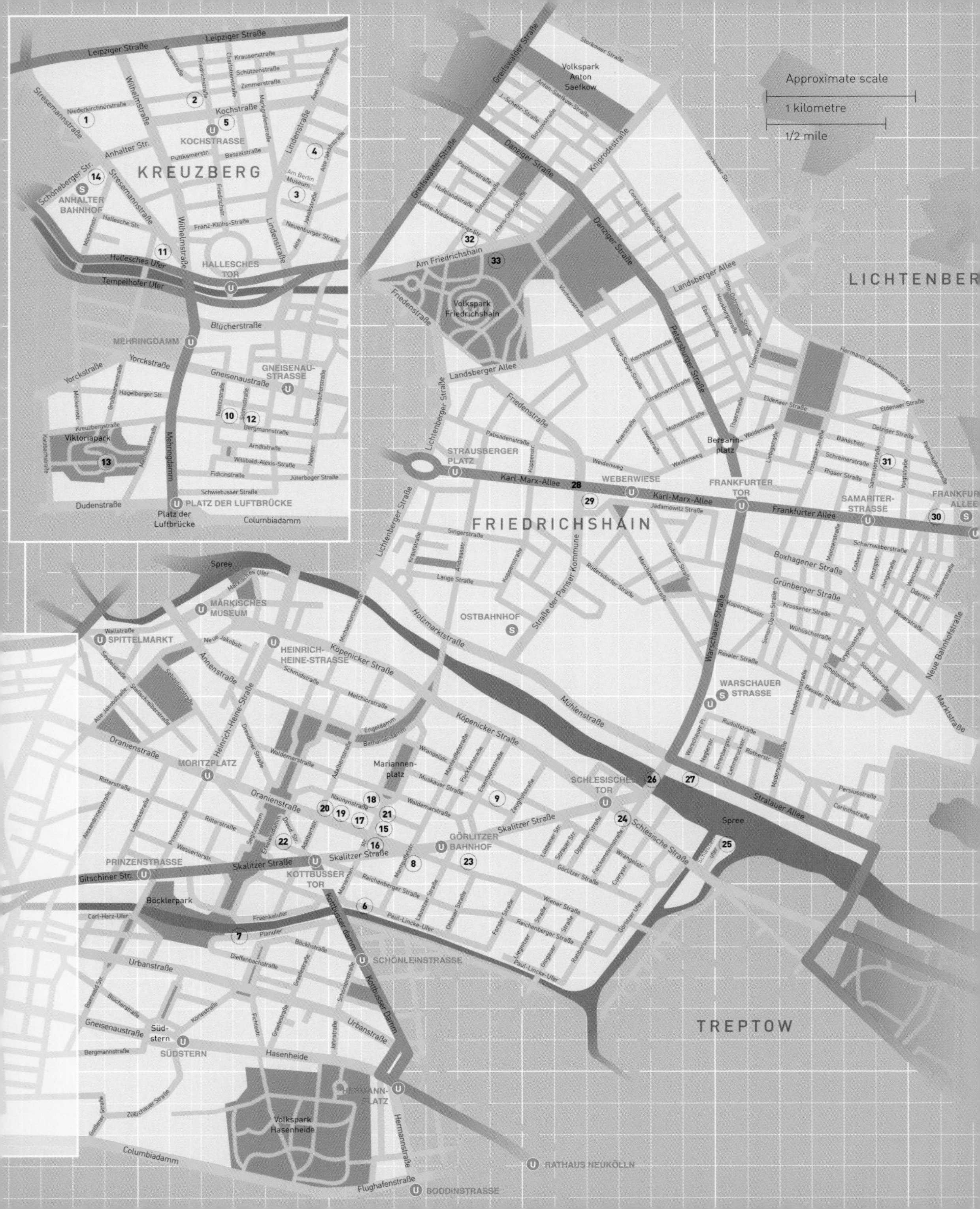

Approximate scale
1 kilometre
1/2 mile
KREUZBERG
Leipziger Straße
Niederkirchnerstraße
Stresemannstraße
Wilhelmstraße
Kochstraße
KOCHSTRASSE
Krausenstraße
Schützenstraße
Zimmerstraße
Friedrichstraße
Charlottenstraße
Markgrafenstraße
Axel-Springer-Straße
Anhalter Str.
Puttkamerstr.
Besselstraße
Lindenstraße
Alte Jakobstraße
Am Berlin Museum
Schöneberger Str.
ANHALTER BAHNHOF
Hallesche Str.
Franz-Klühs-Straße
Neuenburger Straße
Hallesches Ufer
Tempelhofer Ufer
HALLESCHES TOR
Blücherstraße
MEHRINGDAMM
Yorckstraße
Gneisenaustraße
GNEISENAU-STRASSE
Hagelberger Str.
Großbeerenstraße
Möckernstr.
Kreuzbergstraße
Viktoriapark
Bergmannstraße
Arndtstraße
Willibald-Alexis-Straße
Fidicinstraße
Schwiebusser Straße
Jüterboger Straße
Mehringdamm
Dudenstraße
PLATZ DER LUFTBRÜCKE
Platz der Luftbrücke
Columbiadamm
1
2
3
4
5
10
11
12
13
14
Storkower Straße
Volkspark Anton Saefkow
Greifswalder Straße
Danziger Straße
Kniprodestraße
Am Friedrichshain
Volkspark Friedrichshain
Friedenstraße
Landsberger Allee
LICHTENBERG
Petersburger Straße
Hermann-Blankenstein-Straße
Eldenaer Straße
Lichtenberger Straße
STRAUSBERGER PLATZ
Karl-Marx-Allee
WEBERWIESE
FRANKFURTER TOR
Bersarinplatz
Frankfurter Allee
SAMARITER-STRASSE
FRANKFURTER ALLEE
FRIEDRICHSHAIN
Boxhagener Straße
Grünberger Straße
Straße der Pariser Kommune
OSTBAHNHOF
Holzmarktstraße
Mühlenstraße
Warschauer Straße
WARSCHAUER STRASSE
Revaler Straße
Neue Bahnhofstraße
Markstraße
Stralauer Allee
Spree
MÄRKISCHES MUSEUM
SPITTELMARKT
HEINRICH-HEINE-STRASSE
Köpenicker Straße
Annenstraße
Heinrich-Heine-Straße
Oranienstraße
MORITZPLATZ
Mariannenplatz
Skalitzer Straße
GÖRLITZER BAHNHOF
SCHLESISCHES TOR
Schlesische Straße
PRINZENSTRASSE
Gitschiner Str.
KOTTBUSSER TOR
Böcklerpark
Reichenberger Straße
Paul-Lincke-Ufer
Kottbusser Damm
SCHÖNLEINSTRASSE
Urbanstraße
Gneisenaustraße
Südstern
SÜDSTERN
Hasenheide
HERMANNPLATZ
Volkspark Hasenheide
Hermannstraße
Columbiadamm
RATHAUS NEUKÖLLN
Flughafenstraße
BODDINSTRASSE
TREPTOW
6
7
8
9
15
16
17
18
19
20
21
22
23
24
25
26
27
28
29
30
31
32
33

Overlooked by the Kreuzbergdenkmal (mountain cross monument) commemorating the early 19th-century *Befreiungskriege* (wars of liberation from Napoleon) and designed by architectural genius Karl Friedrich Schinkel, Kreuzberg's reputation as a district of social unrest and experiment stems from the 1970s and 1980s, when students fought and saved large parts of this traditional working-class neighbourhood from demolition. Local authorities, fuelled by 1960s city-planning notions that favour the motorist over the pedestrian, designated large swathes of elegant housing for destruction, but opposition led to squatting and demonstrations and ultimately to the alternative lifestyles that culminated in the mélange we see today. Large parts of Kreuzberg were gentrified and its busy shopping streets, lively open-air markets, canalside walks and its main park, the Hasenheide, ensure that it remains a pleasant place to stroll. A politically sedate, thoroughly mixed population of natives and immigrants coexist in an atmosphere of relaxed multiculturalism.

Physically vast and sprawling to the south of the city's new centre, Kreuzberg divides into two parts. Referring to the old postal codes, Berliners call the more staid area around the shopping district of Bergmannstraße 'Kreuzberg 61'. The neighbourhood around Schlesisches Tor, 'Kreuzberg 36', has an edgier and sharply pronounced anti-bourgeois ethic. Both quarters are essentially urban and residential, but interrupted by charming pockets of artistic culture.

A recent cultural focal point for the area is architect Daniel Libeskind's Jewish Museum (p. 60), which has attracted international attention for its innovative design and the way in which it presents Jewish life throughout the centuries in Berlin. Close to the Potsdamer Platz is an area of concentrated history, containing the Martin-Gropius-Bau Museum (p. 60), behind it the Third Reich's security police headquarters, and on the same plot of land remains of the Wall and the infamous Checkpoint Charlie, once the crossing point between the capitalist and Communist worlds.

Where Checkpoint Charlie once marked division, the Oberbaumbrücke (p. 71), crossing the Spree river and linking Kreuzberg to the former east German district of Friedrichshain, is a potent symbol of the city's reunion. Merged with Kreuzberg after the city's restructuring, the inevitable regeneration of Friedrichshain provides a pleasing contrast to the historically charged sections of Kreuzberg. In the area mainly around the Boxhagener Platz, dozens of bohemian cafés, small creative boutiques and second-hand markets have sprouted up, and on the Friedrichshain riverbank a new line of river terraces are being developed, offering spectacular views of Kreuzberg's turn-of-the-century waterfront loft and office buildings and new destinations for savvy visitors.

AXIS OF EVIL

1 Martin-Gropius-Bau Topographie des Terrors

Stresemannstraße 110/Niederkirchnerstraße 8

Not to be confused with his more famous Bauhaus nephew, Walter, Martin Gropius was so inspired by the Victoria & Albert Museum in London that he built this exhibition space in 1881. For many years it was the 'guardian' of works that were later moved to the Jewish Museum and of Berlin's own art collection, which was given its own home at the Berlinische Galerie (p. 63) in 2004. This has left Martin-Gropius-Bau free to house the contemporary exhibitions for which it is becoming well known. Nearby, in a piece of flat waste ground, lies the excavated Topographie des Terrors, once the site of a cluster of buildings that were at the centre of the Nazi regime, including Prinz-Albrecht Straße 8, which was the Gestapo headquarters and the Prinz Albrecht Palais, where the SS leadership was based, making this area the government district of the Third Reich and the location from which the horrors of the Holocaust were masterminded. Reconstruction of buildings to house the documentation centre, plus a stretch of Berlin Wall that is also standing here, is estimated to be finished in 2005.

HISTORY IN THE MAKING

2 Café Adler

TWO MILLENNIA OF GERMAN JEWISH HISTORY

3 Jüdisches Museum

Lindenstraße 9–14

After a tour of the lower ground floor of the Jewish Museum, visitors could be forgiven for thinking they have come to the Daniel Libeskind Museum, so palpable is the architect's signature in the building-memorial design. But no one can deny that the New York–based creator of the World Trade Center master plan has succeeded in capturing an ineffable degree of emotion in a museum that was bound to be controversial from the outset. The interior of the deconstructivist, zinc-clad building compresses confusion and alienation: the dark concrete Holocaust Tower is an architectural emulation of a gas chamber; the Memory Void is a sad, weighted place for silent meditation; the dense concrete-columned Garden of Exile evokes the suffering of the Jewish experience. The museum exhibition itself celebrates Jewish–German life in a walk through history.

MADNESS

HOME SWEET HOME

4 Berlinische Galerie

Alte Jakobstraße 124–28

With a collection of Berlin art that dates back to 1870, it is strange that the Berlinische Galerie has never had its own home. The idea for one collection originated in 1975, when curators felt there was no cohesion among the large number of 20th-century pieces that were dispersed in several local museums. For many years parts of the collection were displayed at the Martin-Gropius-Bau (p. 60), but construction work on the 3,600-square-metre (38,750-square-foot) former glass factory began in May 2003 so that the 10,000 works on paper could finally be given a home of their own. The focus is on early Modernism, Neue Sachlichkeit, Expressionism and Dadaism as well as the art of East Berlin.

SALT AND TOBACCO

5 Sale e Tabacchi

WATER WITHIN

6 Paul-Lincke-Ufer

- Schuhtanten, no. 44
- Café am Ufer, no. 42

Along the banks of this canal, which marks the border with Neukölln, are several shops and cafés forming a little new enclave in this corner of Kreuzberg. Kerstin Angela Sowada studied fashion and Michaela Fischer interior design, and in 2000 they decided to pool their resources and open Schuhtanten ('Shoe Aunts'), a store selling Italian shoes for men and women and a quirky selection of hats and clothes. There are pieces by Danish NOA NOA, hats by Berlin-based König Walter and some of their own skirts and dresses. Several cafés overlook the water serving all-day breakfasts and an ever-increasing number of boutiques. Proximity to the Tuesday and Friday Türkischer Markt by the Maybachufer makes this a delightful place for a canalside stroll and a peaceful place for post-market relaxation.

A WELCOME PORT

7 Iskele

Gegenüber Planufer 82

Built in 1904, this is the oldest ship restaurant in Europe, according to Turkish owner Mustafa Yilmaz, who turned it into an original Aegean dining salon in 2000. The boat has been docked at this spot for a quarter of a century, and Yilmaz is proud to have made it a genuine family-run business. He studied catering and management but learnt to cook from his mother and grandmother; his mother works at the restaurant alongside his wife, sister and brother-in-law. Every Friday morning his uncle in Izmir (on Turkey's western coast) buys fish at the market and by mid-afternoon the next day it is ready to serve in Iskele, whose name in Turkish means 'little harbour'. Yilmaz cooks in a pure Aegean style: his pike fillet with herbs, roasted onions, pine nuts, tomatoes and red peppers is the house speciality. With over 25 choices, he boasts a huge selection of cold appetizers (and there are also fifteen warm ones). In the summer of 2004 they celebrated the ship's centenary with live music up on deck.

SUNNY SIDE UP

8 Cafe Morgenland

Skalitzer Straße 35

There is a German saying: *Die Augen sind größer als der Magen*, which is a version of 'the eyes are always bigger than the stomach'. This maxim is never more apt than when faced with a buffet, and the one at Morgenland is a veritable food mountain. Berlin's favourite meal, the all-day breakfast, is available here as a continuously restocked, never-ending eat-as-much-as-you-like/can buffet. German and French cheeses, Italian and Spanish sausages, eggs in all variations, quark (a creamy curd cheese), yogurt, cereals, muesli, pasta, gratins, home-made marmalade, jams, honey, fruits and pickles. To wash it all down, choose coffee, tea, juice, water or a champagne mixer. To mop up the mess, there is always freshly baked bread and *Brötchen* (breakfast rolls). One should reserve before going.

ONE MORE TIME

9 Abendmahl

Muskauer Straße 9

The food and atmosphere in chef-owner Udo Einenkel's crazy camp creation are flaming, flashy and flamboyant. Abendmahl means 'The Last Supper', only the beginning of the kitsch religious icons that abound here. The off-the-beaten-track vegetarian and fish restaurant sells organic beer alongside a menu that offers the most curious of dishes, which might look familiar when they arrive, but Einenkel has given each of them a special name that sets them apart: 'Flaming Inferno' is a Thai fish curry; 'Affair Emma Peel' is a mascarpone and melon mousse. Einenkel's love of food art extends to desserts: 'Heavenly Suicide' features an edible white snowman and 'Cold War' a huge ice-cream igloo; there is even a 'Butterfly Blossom Sorbet', featuring wild-rose petals, an innovative ingredient that Einenkel uses generously in season. 'Flaming Inferno' aptly characterizes Abendmahl itself.

MEDITERRANEAN SPECIALITIES

10 Knofi

Bergmannstraße 98

This is a deli at its best. Berlin has a huge Turkish population (it is sometimes referred to as the world's fifth largest Turkish city), many of whom are settled in Kreuzberg. While the Türkischer Markt by the Maybachufer has on sale such staples as olives, bread and vegetables every Tuesday and Friday, Knofi is open all week, and owner Senay Celik's recipe has proved so popular that he now has three stores, all in Kreuzberg. This, the first, opened in 1986. The shops are decorated with food: aubergines, red and orange paprika and fat, round pepperoni sausages hang on ropes from the ceiling, producing a pungent hunger-inducing aroma that pervades the air. Bean pastes, hummus, tzatziki, cheeses soaking in their own oils, fresh pastas and Knofi's own speciality artichoke paste are all freshly home-made daily.

MASTER THEATRE

11 Hebbel-Theater

Stresemannstraße 29

This theatre was the first commission for Oskar Kaufmann, who became one of the most prolific theatre builders of his time, responsible for six in Berlin alone (including the Volksbühne in 1914 (p. 156), and the Theater am Ku'damm in 1921). In 1933 he fled to Palestine when the National Socialist party came to power, and there he built Tel Aviv's famous Hebrew Theatre Habima. The Hebbel-Theater's story began in 1908, when the theatre's founder, Eugen Robert, took a chance on a then inexperienced Kaufmann, who repaid him with a magnificent mahogany Jugendstil auditorium, which opened with a performance of Friedrich Hebbel's *Maria Magdalena*, and exists to this day, despite numerous owners and bankruptcy. It became a listed monument in 1979 and is protected by a preservation order. It is known today for a programme of in-house productions and touring guest performances.

EYE CANDY

12 Aquamarin

Bergmannstraße 20

Lucie Schnurrer's jewelry store is in reality a gallery specializing in art for the body. At any given time she displays the work of over twenty designers and further decorates the walls with changing mini-shows. Her artists are predominantly German, although a few are Swiss – 'but none is ordinary!' she points out. Schnurrer sells pieces by Ute Dippel, who paints enamel on to metal to create delicate flowers, glass jewels by Andrea Borst and Ulrike Reh's silver pebble rings. Monica Jacubec had the novel idea of adding acrylic to a silver ring, which flips over to allow the wearer to customize the piece with her own flower or photo. Schnurrer is associated with the Bundesverband Kunsthandwerk (part of the Arts and Crafts Council), and whether the jewelry is crafted from wool, wood or mother-of-pearl, each piece is a unique design expression.

CROSS TOWN; NO TRAFFIC

13 Viktoriapark

Bounded by Kreuzbergstraße, Methfesselstraße and Katzbachstraße

The literal translation of Kreuzberg is 'cross mountain', referring to the cross that stands at the top of a steep hill that forms Viktoriapark. The cross, a memorial designed by Karl Friedrich Schinkel in 1821 to commemorate the German victories in the Napoleonic Wars, is just one symbol of the celebratory theme continued throughout the neighbourhood in the streets named after generals and battles. Covered in gnarled trees and with a breathtaking waterfall that cascades from the cross down to street level, the hill is wild and romantic. Only after a hard trek up sharply twisting steep paths to the summit do you see that all around is man-made: the disused Schultheiss brewery sits on its rear slopes, slowly being converted into housing. The vista over the city is amazing, an energizing reward for the taxing climb.

OUT OF BODY, OUT OF THIS WORLD

14 Liquidrom at the Tempodrom

Möckernstraße 10

A new way to Nirvana is what Liquidrom at the Tempodrom is offering. Brainchild of Irene Moessinger, who once had her cultural and music performance stage where the chancellor now has his office, Tempodrom has long been a German institution. In 1995 Moessinger founded this new venue, comprising a large and small arena and the surreal Liquidrom. 'As the Tempodrom revitalizes the circus tent, so the Liquidrom invigorates the thermal bath' was the idea behind a spaceship-like building that houses a warm saltwater pool, saunas and steam baths and relaxation areas. But this is no ordinary pool: the Liquidrom is infused with sound, and as bathers sink into the water they are immersed in an aural aquarium created by liquid-sound developer Micky Remann, who has designed a programme of underwater music and light installations that feature a classical night on Fridays and DJ mixes on Saturdays. The bath is open every day from 10 a.m. until 10 p.m. or midnight on Fridays and Saturdays, and, as you might expect, the atmosphere and clientele change throughout the day. Massages and treatments are available, and there are live performances to accompany the experience at every full moon, when Liquidrom stays open until 2 a.m.

BE STILL, MY BEATING HEART

15 Rote Harfe/Orient Lounge

FOOD AND PHILOSOPHY

16 Kafka

Oranienstraße 204

Situated in the most multicultural area of Kreuzberg, Kafka's Turkish–German owner offers international cuisine along with philosophy. Lamb, fish, beef, and vegetarian dishes reflect his own influences plus the more 'right-on' demands of his local clientele. One of its features is a delightful little beergarden that overlooks a busy street corner. Kafka is popular as a starting point for long nights out in Kreuzberg (which frequently happen thanks to the abundance of watering holes in the vicinity) and a choice destination for Sunday brunch in summer – get there early for a space in the garden.

ROW, ROW, ROW YOUR BOAT

17 Bateau Ivre

Oranienstraße 18

Named after a poem by French poet Arthur Rimbaud, this café has always been known as a sanctuary for intellectuals, thinkers and writers, and as most tend to be self-employed, it is pretty much full all day long. Bateau Ivre keeps its prices low to draw the hordes of hungry bohemians into the 'drunken ship'. Coloured paper lanterns dance merrily from rope strung across the dining room, while wooden floors and natural hues on the walls create a down-to-earth backdrop to higher-level discussion. Choices from the kitchen vary, but thick soups and stews are common, and many have a Moroccan influence. Calm music, relaxed staff and bright, light views from its two corner windows make it a popular local den.

BATH-TIME

18 Schokoladenfabrik

Mariannenstraße 6

Run for women by women, Schokoladenfabrik is an oasis of calm and authenticity. Most European spas and saunas are open-minded, no-nonsense places to relax, but in this hammam, like those in Turkey whence it gets its name, time is taken to cleanse and gossip. An entrance below ground leads to a carpeted tearoom, where cakes and fruit can be enjoyed in front of a warming stove. The tiled steamy hammam itself is lit from above, and visitors mix water to the desired temperature in individual marble basins before lying down on the *göbek tasi* (heated raised platform) in the centre of the room. A sauna and temptingly inexpensive massages can be booked for 20- to 60-minute time slots to complete the experience.

STRING ISLAND

19 Fadeninsel

Oranienstraße 23

Marita Tenberg is enjoying the glow of an international knitting renaissance. Her shop pays homage to the handicraft with balls of every shade and mix of every imaginable colour. Traditional threads, cashmere, mohair, angora and pure wool now compete with microfibre, cotton, silk, viscose, rayon and pure washable – the bright young Turks of the knitting world. Tenberg and her colleagues are always knitting themselves: their gloves, slippers, stripy tights, hats and sweaters are available in-store. The ever-popular Pulswärmer (wrist warmers), more a necessity than a fashion statement in below-freezing Berlin winters, are crafted in felted wool. Tenberg says she will make anything to order if the time and price are right, and for those with itchier knitting fingers there is a vast range of patterns for sale.

THE IMAGINARY FACTORY

20 Die Imaginäre Manufaktur (DIM)

CLEARLY SIMPLE

21 Lucid 21

Mariannenstraße 50

Italian designer Luis Gunsch and Austrian artist Sylvia Kranawetvogl started working together as fashion designers under the Lucid 21 banner in the summer of 2002. 'Our clothes are colourful and cute, but also pop and arty. We like minimal simple cuts.' Often inspired by fairy tales, their upbeat attitude is expressed in the prints that appear on many of their garments. Their boutique is tiny, with powder-puff pink and cream the predominant tones. Gunsch and Kranawetvogl admit that their location in less affluent Kreuzberg means that they are somewhat off the beaten fashion track, but they design and make everything themselves, producing unique originals, an apt reflection of the street style that dominates trendy young Berlin. 'We are not inspired by particular big names: we would prefer to be "small heroes" for other young designers trying to make it on their own.'

IVG
SCHW
FREI

CHEESE TREES

22 Würgeengel

MAÑANA MAÑANA

23 Morena

Wiener Straße 60

The Spanish name of the bar reflects a Mediterranean attitude toward having a good time. It is a classic Kreuzberg hang-out, decorated in a kaleidoscopic mosaic of tiles that recalls the feel of the distant warm south. During the lunch-hour the place livens up with locals, who meet to chat and drink red wine, an activity that usually continues well into the afternoon, the red giving way to rosé and spirits. By the evening Morena is once again transformed into a full-on bar with cocktails and hard liquor enjoyed by the musicians, artists and former squatters who make up the local community.

UNDERWATER LOVE

24 Cream & Watergate

PIER LIFE

25 Der Freischwimmer

Vor dem Schlesischen Tor 2a

Since 1932 this old pier jutting out over the Flutgraben river has been the place where punters and rowers have come to hire craft for their water antics. During the Communist era, the pier's location along the East-West divide meant the river was usually still under the eyes of guards who might shoot to kill anyone who tried to cross it in search of political freedom. Along the eastern banks sprouted *Schrebergarten* (allotments), where nature-hungry city-dwellers could enjoy a waterside vista. Today a beer garden on the pier caters for all climes and temperaments.

CROSSING THE DIVIDE

26 Oberbaumbrücke East Side Gallery

Mühlenstraße

Providing views from Mitte to Treptow and connecting Kreuzberg with Friedrichshain across the River Spree, this spectacular neo-Gothic bridge dates back to 1892. Architect Otto Stahn built it to resemble a fortified town gate and decorated it with cross-shaped vaults, coats of arms and two 34-metre (111-foot-high) towers. It also marks one end of the largest open-air gallery in the world, the longest stretch of Wall still in one piece, which has been designated a listed monument. After the Wall came down in 1989, 118 artists from 21 countries decorated it. The East Side Gallery opened in 1990 and stretches 1,316 metres (4,317 feet) from the Ostbahnhof. Restored in 2000, it features work by Gerhard Lahr, who drew *Berlin–New York*, Dmitri Vrubel's *Brotherly Kiss* and *Fatherland* by Günther Schäfer.

NUMERICAL VALUES

27 Q3A & Club 12/34

A ROAD BY ANY OTHER NAME

28 Karl-Marx-Allee

From Alexanderplatz to Frankfurter Tor

This is the apogee of Communist architecture: a processional allee nearly 90 metres (300 feet) wide – purpose-built to double as an aircraft landing strip – stretching southeast from Alexanderplatz as far as the eye can see, flanked by a seemingly never-ending white stretch of public housing (which is often referred to as the 'wedding cake'). This was a Soviet dream, and until 1961 the street was known as Stalinallee in tribute to the leader of the era who had instigated the project. Once built, the residences were homes to the most important party members of the East German capital. Five architects worked on the oversized project, the best remembered being Herman Henselmann. On 17 June 1953 the street became the focus of a workers' insurrection, which was suppressed only by military intervention, reminders of which are provided to today's pedestrians in 39 information posts, starting at Strausberger Platz, that provide a historical, architectural and geographical tour.

BARFLY

29 CSA Bar

NEW TALENT NOW

30 Berlinomat

RED OCTOBER

31 Anastasia

Samariterstraße 13

The name gives it away. A Russian restaurant located on a sunny corner, Anastasia offers no clue that it is owned by young Turk Ayhan Celik, whose only Russian connection is that his family hailed from near Erzincan, not so far from the former Soviet border. He opened Anastia to appeal to former East Berliners, who were familiar with dishes such as borscht (beetroot soup), *pelmini* (a Russian meat-stuffed tortellini), *wareniki* (the vegetarian version) and *soljanka* (invented for a hungry tsar who came home late one night and his cook was forced to use the leftovers of all the other dishes to rustle up this soup). Blinis come as a savoury dish (with caviar) or dessert (accompanied by yogurt or compote).

BREAD AND ROSES

32 Brot und Rosen

139

VIENNESE MODERNE

33 Café Schönbrunn

Am Schwanenteich, im Volkspark, Friedrichshain 8

Drawing inspiration from the café culture so prevalent in Vienna, owners Hille Saw and Matthias Petsche chose the name of the city's famous castle for their eatery when it opened in its pleasant setting in 2000. Niki Winkelmayer is the architect behind the café's hip interior, but it is the 1960s space-age pavilion set amid the leafy greenery of Friedrichshain Park that sets it apart. Dishes tend toward the more traditional: Wiener Schnitzel with potato salad and gherkins on the side is an ever-popular order.

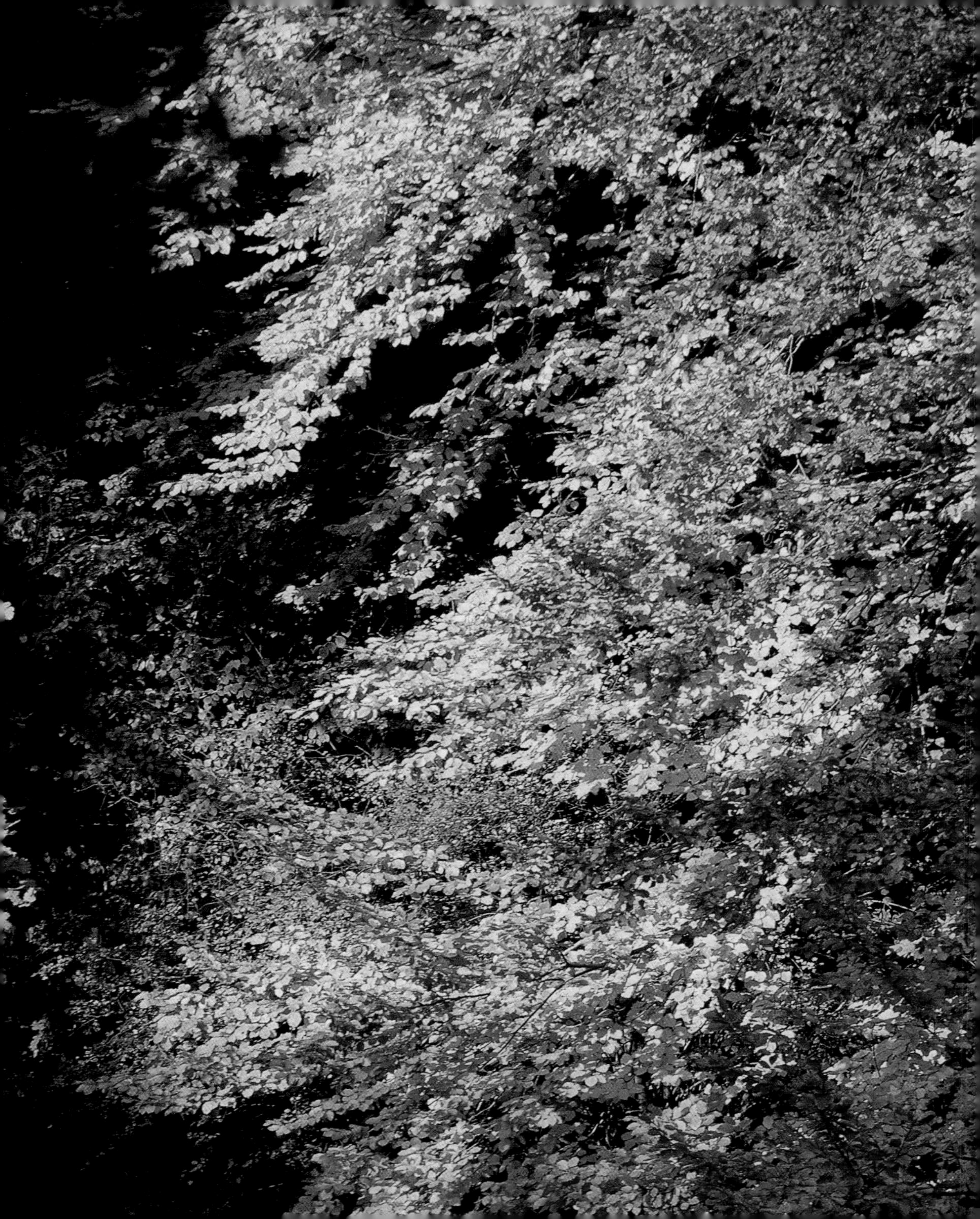

Schöneberg
Tiergarten

Approximate scale
1 kilometre
1/2 mile
TURMSTRASSE
Alt-Moabit
Essener Straße
Stromstraße
Kirchstraße
Thomasiusstraße
Calvinstraße
Paulstraße
Invalidenstraße
Spree
Holsteiner Ufer
Heligoländer Ufer
Bundesratufer
Lessingstraße
Levetzowstraße
Franklinstraße
Agricolastraße
Wikingerufer
Wullenweberstraße
Hansa-Ufer
BELLEVUE
Flensburger Straße
Lüneburger Straße
Werftstraße
Willy-Brandt-Str.
HANSAPLATZ
Bartningallee
Bellevue Ufer
Haus der Kulturen der Welt
Entlastungsstraße
Englischer Garten
Schloßpark Bellevue
John-Foster-Dulles-Allee
Kurfürsten Platz
Altonaer Straße
Klopstockstraße
Händelallee
Spreeweg
Bellevueallee
Bachstraße
Marchstraße
Salzufer
Einsteinufer
TIERGARTEN
Siegessäule
Straße des 17. Juni
Ernst-Reuter-Platz
Rosengarten
TIERGARTEN
Großer Weg
Große Sternallee
Hofjägerallee
Neuer See
Müller-Breslau-Straße
Hardenbergstraße
Fasanenstraße
Lichtensteinallee
Tiergartenstraße
Zoologischer Garten
Steinplatz
Jebensstraße
Stülerstraße
Klingelhöferstraße
Hiroshimastraße
Hildebrandstraße
Stauffenbergstraße
Sigismundstraße
ZOOLOGISCHER GARTEN
Budapester Straße
Corneliusstraße
Von-der-Heydt-Straße
Reichpietschufer
CHARLOTTENBURG
Kantstraße
Lützowufer
Keithstraße
Lützowplatz
Wichmannstraße
Schöneberger Ufer
KURFÜRSTENDAMM
Nürnberger Str.
Kurfürstenstraße
Lützowstraße
Magdeburger Platz
Joachimstaler Straße
Rankestraße
Marburger Straße
Tauentzienstraße
Ansbacher Straße
Bayreuther Straße
Schillstraße
Einemstraße
Derfflingerstraße
Genthiner Straße
Kluckstraße
Am Karlsbad
Bissingzeile
Augsburger Straße
Eisenacher Str.
WITTENBERG PLATZ
Passauer Straße
Pohlstraße
Potsdamer Straße
Körnerstraße
Flottwellstraße
AUGSBURGER STRASSE
Kleiststraße
Lietzenburger Straße
Martin-Luther-Straße
KURFÜRSTENSTRASSE
Bundesallee
Spichernstraße
Fuggerstraße
NOLLENDORFPLATZ
GLEISDREIECK
Geisbergstraße
VIKTORIA-LUISE-PLATZ
Motzstraße
Nollendorfstraße
Bülowstraße
SPICHERNSTRASSE
Winterfeldtstraße
BÜLOWSTRASSE
Regensburger Straße
Goltzstraße
Gleditschstraße
Nachodstraße
Luitpoldstraße
Hohenstaufenstraße
Pallasstraße
Steinmetzstraße
Möckernstraße
Bamberger Str.
Frankenstraße
Goebenstraße
Barbarossastraße
Münchener Straße
Heinrich-von-Kleist-Park
YORCKSTRASSE
Yorckstraße
GÜNTZELSTRASSE
Güntzelstraße
Aschaffenburger Straße
Freisinger Straße
Rosenheimer Straße
Großgörschenstraße
Prinzregentenstraße
KLEISTPARK
Grunewaldstraße
BAYERISCHER PLATZ
EISENACHER STRASSE
Wilmanndamm
Crellestraße
Bautzener Straße
Berliner Straße
Apostel-Paulus-Straße
Vorbergstraße
Langenscheidtstraße
BERLINER STRASSE
Wartburg Platz
Wartburgstraße
Akazienstraße
Helmstr.
Kreuzbergstraße
Viktoriapark
Meraner Straße
Innsbrucker Straße
Salzburger Straße
Monumentenstraße
SCHÖNEBERG
Badenschestraße
Meininger Str.
Belziger Straße
Hauptstraße
Katzbachstraße
H.-Lassen-Park
RATHAUS SCHÖNEBERG
Kolonnenstraße
Dudenstraße
Dominicusstraße
1
2
3
4
5
6
7
8
9
10
11
12
13
14
15
16
17
18
19
20

Once a royal hunting ground, Tiergarten's leafy southern edge was settled by wealthy Berliners, many of whose dwellings were later turned into embassies. Today the surrounding neighbourhood is an interesting mix of residences, museums and embassies. Running through its heart is Potsdamer Straße, which has resisted gentrification throughout its existence and now boasts a profusion of quirky nightclubs, restaurants and Turkish shops that spill their wares out on to the street. Mirroring the cultural and institutional diversity of the area, the banks of the Lützowkanal are lined with an array of buildings from different eras, including the post-modern Kunstgeschichtsbibliothek, the former Reichspostamt from the Third Reich, apartment houses dating from the early 1900s and shiny modern embassies, residential constructions and parks that add their own colours to the city's canvas.

To the south, the Schöneberg district is best reflected in the charming, bustling street life of the *Platze*s and streets. In the summer, packed markets form an artistic and creative backdrop for cultivated alternative lifestyles. Wander along Nollendorfplatz and Winterfeldtplatz all the way to Goltzstraße and Akazienstraße, and stray off the main roads to discover the quaint Viktoria-Luise-Platz (p. 78), delightful cafés, restaurants, boutiques and shops. A special event is the Saturday Winterfeldtmarkt (p. 83), where an assortment of daily goods makes an attractive display, further animated by nearby cafés and restaurants. Berliners tend to cease work at the slightest excuse: even a fine day will bring people out into this urban playground to eat at the early bars and breakfast cafés and shop at the market. Nudged up against this area is the largely gay quarter, with its bars and cafés stuffed full with people of every proclivity – a cherished legacy of Berlin's Roaring Twenties.

All these quarters flow into each other and make for a pleasant stroll through this dense urban area. Although Schöneberg has many examples of modern architecture, it is largely defined by grand 19th-century *Altbauen*, with their voluptuous ornaments and daring cantilevering balconies. Signs displaying the names of famous artists, politicians and actors who once lived and created here are constant reminders of the area's rich cultural heritage. Between Eisenacher Straße and Winterfeldtplatz, for example, Christopher Isherwood, author of the book *Goodbye to Berlin*, which was later made into the movie *Cabaret* with Liza Minelli, lived here in the 1920s; David Bowie and Iggy Pop spent many years around Kleistpark. Schöneberg's main roads are mostly long, small-scale shopping parades that run north–south and, like Eisenacher Straße, Potsdamer Straße and Akazienstraße, gradually change character from bohemian to ethnic.

WATER WORLD

1 Aquarium

Budapester Straße 32

Enter a world of silent blue. Eerie lights shine through tanks of water, projecting aqueous shadows on stone floors. A musty, damp scent hangs heavy in the moist warm air. This is the sensory experience that is Berlin's Aquarium, located in the grounds of Germany's first zoo, the 1844 Zoologischer Garten, designed by Martin Lictenstein and Peter Joseph Lenné. The aquarium was built in 1911–13 to plans drawn up by curator and director Oskar Heinroth, and today the aquarium houses over 500 types of ocean life, fish, reptiles and insects. The larger tanks are on the ground floor, some containing the world's most successfully bred-in-captivity swarms of pink, blue and clear jellyfish. Upstairs lazy crocodiles and alligators are the slothful residents of a humid hothouse.

A ROOM WITH A VIEW

2 Hugos

136

DIPLOMATS 'R' US

3 Embassy District

Tiergartenstraße

When the capital of Germany returned to Berlin, so did the foreign embassies. Many countries used the opportunity to sponsor major international architecture competitions to make their mark on the city. While the French, Russian and British embassies rest in prime locations around the Brandenburg Gate, many embassies took up residence along Tiergartenstraße, a stretch that flanks the Tiergarten's southern edge. Indian, Italian and Japanese embassies are all installed in imposing free-standing buildings. The Nordic states combined forces in a recent architecturally celebrated diplomatic centre on the Klingelhöfer triangle. Next door, the Mexican embassy shines like an Aztec jewel. But it is the overall diversity of styles that makes a wander along these façades so appealing. Tiergartenstraße also houses impressive representations of the federal states of Brandenburg, Mecklenburg–Western Pomerania, Hesse, Lower Saxony and Saarland.

FOUNTAIN OF LIFE

4 Viktoria-Luise Platz

Motzsraße and Winterfeldtstraße

A rarity in Berlin: Viktoria-Luise Platz is special today because it is one of the few old squares in Berlin untouched by bombing during the Second World War. Its classic design is the work of Fritz Encke, a leading landscape architect when he created it in 1898. Named after the daughter of German Emperor Wilhelm II, it has evolved today into a mini-arcade of hip restaurants and cafés, shops, hairdressers and bars, facing onto or along the roads that lead into the square. Covered in trees and dotted by old-fashioned lamps and a fountain, the park's west side was recently pedestrianized, helping to reawaken the aura of a bygone era.

PAN ASIAN

5 Shima

Schwäbische Straße 5

When Ernesto Kuoni opened Shima in 1998, no one in Berlin had heard of pan-Asian cuisine. 'I had travelled all over the world,' Kuoni explains, 'and I wanted to do something healthy that mixed it all up.' Kuoni hails from Switzerland and does not profess to be trained in the nuances of any particular form of Asian cooking, but he travelled the world (including a stint as cabin crew member aboard the Orient Express) before settling in Berlin in 1991. 'What I can do is take elements of Indian, Vietnamese and Thai and interpret it in a European style of my own imagination.' He certainly plays the culinary field: the 'Sense of Shima' appetizer is a Japanese plate with tandoori beef fillet and tapioca garnished with lemon grass and herbs. There are curries, jungle chicken and marlin Nori rolls all on one menu, constituting a veritable cornucopia of Pacific Rim flavours, which in the northern European context is a breath of fresh exotica. Artist Detlef Schulz installed the crazy leopard-print lounge and bar.

MORE THAN A BIRD

6 Storch

134

BEER BARREL

7 Felsenkeller

146

CHOCOLATE FACTORY

8 Chocolaterie Estrellas

170

AQUA

THANKSGIVING

9 Gottlob

Akazienstraße 17

Overlooked by the impressive Apostel-Paulus Kirche, the little café-restaurant Gottlob ('praise be to God') serves fare that is energizing and wholesome. Owners Jörg Grundmann and Dirk Thürnagel installed beautiful glass wall lamps and chandeliers taken from an old Berlin hotel, painted the cornices in red and gold, tiled the floor with slate and made a Déco bar with a built-in cake display to create a dusty-decadent décor. In warmer months the garden, with its elegant wrought-iron railings, is crowded with diners who have come to eat orange and carrot soup or salads with roasted sunflower seeds and avocado. Encouraged by the success of Gottlob, the duo have opened another café, Feuerbach, in the south of the city.

SOUTHERN FLAVOUR

10 Südwind

Akazienstraße 7

It was the result of frequent travels to Tuscany that made husband and wife Mike and Astrid Peacock decide to bring their favourite delicacies back to Berlin, at first to sell wholesale, later on at a stall and finally at Südwind. The scent of quality organic delicatessen hits you the moment you walk through the door. A large vitrine is filled with Serrano, Parma, Tuscan and other varieties of air-dried ham and sausages. 'We are very proud to sell organic sausages from the island of Rügen and fresh goat's cheese in a glass with oil and garlic from the coast of the Ostsee,' says Astrid Peacock. 'The aim is not to sell only Mediterranean products but anything that is good. We are always on the lookout for hand-made products from smaller producers, as you can really taste the difference.' Goods can be sampled in Café Sur, opened next door to allow customers to try the fresh pasta or antipasti straight away.

MAY, JUNE, JULY

11 April

Winterfeldtstraße 56

Andreas Strohschein owns this delightful restaurant and the next-door wine shop Vinum. His family-friendly attitude to dining is apparent from a specially designed children's playroom built to one side of the main dining area. The street-side space is more informal, with a long bar and cake-display cabinet; tables at the back are covered in white linen and present Strohschein's educated wine recommendations, imparting a bistro quality to the ambience. His menu features a selection of pizzas and pastas and a huge breakfast selection, which, served on giant square platters so large they almost resemble trays, are meals in themselves. The monthly-changing breakfast special can be quite unusual, having recently featured an Asian menu of wasabi cream dip and tofu marinated in soya-oyster sauce and sweet chilies, all washed down with a mango lassi.

SHAPE + FORM

12 Herz + Stöhr

Winterfeldtstraße 52

Sabina Herz and Anja Stöhr's designs for women reflect their adaptation of philosopher Immanuel Kant: 'It is better to be a fool in fashion than to be out of fashion.' The two women formed their label in 1995, opening a shop 1997. The ensuing years have seen them gain fame and prestige, with such high-profile clients as actresses Veronica Ferres and Daniela Lunkewitz and ice-skating champion Katharina Witt. The shop space, a former bakery, doubles as their atelier, so items can be altered or remodelled in the back. 'Our fashion derives from an exploration of colour and form,' explains Stohr, 'which are expressions of sexy, feminine shapes.' This is apparent from their continuous line of dresses, which hold their dynamic form even on the hanger. Shirt dresses from non-shirt textiles are a signature style and connect their sporty daywear to evening glamour lines.

Meyers
Konversations-
Lexikon
15
Meyers
Konversations-
Lexikon
17
Meyers
Konversations-
Lexikon
18

WHAT'S BEHIND?

13 Green Door

PURE FOOD AND FLOWERS

14 Winterfeldtmarkt

Winterfeldtplatz

One of Berlin's liveliest street markets, Winterfeldtmarkt is where the locals go for their Saturday-morning shopping, returning home laden with baskets of fresh produce. Stallholders come into the city from the country to sell organic fruit and vegetables; olives with garlic, with oil, with anchovies or simply plain; wholegrain, dark, light and white breads are freshly baked. The flowersellers are worth a visit, especially if you come to the market just before it closes in the late afternoon when, with a little haggling, prices are reduced by up to 80%. As it is illegal in Germany for stallholders to bellow out their best deals, it can be entertaining to listen out for the novel ways that *Marktschreier* (market criers) attract customers' attention.

HOUSE OF CARDS

15 Café Einstein

Kurfürstenstraße 58

Until its incarnation as Café Einstein, this stately house on a quiet, tree-lined street had a wild history. Originally built as a private residence in 1876, it became the home of silent-movie actress Henny Porten, who was later blacklisted by the Nazis when she married a Jew. In the 1920s, in a mirrored room behind the library, the salons became home to an illegal casino where all Berlin gambled. The Nazis shut down the illicit activity, yet this was the only building on the street that was not raised to the ground by the Allies' bombs. After Porten's death in 1955, the descendants of the original owners of the Café Einstein, which was located on Unter den Linden during the 1920s, bought the house, which they ran as a café until 1978. Today Elisabeth Andraschko and her husband own this Berlin institution and paean to the Viennese café, with the mouth-watering smell of *Apfelstrudel* among the many experiences that await visitors. A classic.

ALL FOR ONE AND ONE FOR ALL

16 Kumpelnest 3000

CIVILIZED SEDUCTION

17 Victoria Bar

Potsdamer Straße 102

Some may find this is an unusual location for a sophisticated drinking experience. Potsdamerstraße has been a bit of a backwater since the 1920s, withstanding numerous municipal makeover attempts. But owners Stefan Weber, Kerstin Ehmer and Beate Hindermann saw through the grime to what is also a very geographically accessible part of Berlin's city centre. Visitors should be aware that despite the central accessibility of location, entry is not ensured unless dress sense is not up to scratch. Shortly after its opening in 2001, Victoria won an award for its leather banquettes, long stretch bar, natural wood and dark wall tones, all the work of designer 'Kalle' Ingo Strobel and painter Thomas Hauser.

ALMOST BOILING

18 90 Grad

Dennewitzstraße 37

Berlin's sexy answer to the faded ideology of Studio 54: a huge, glamorous nightclub packed with divas and their heroes has been the place to be seen since it opened in 1989. The front-runners of the party circuit in those days were Bob Young, Britt Kanja and Hille Saul, who sprinkled their magic party dust all over the hothouse. When celebrities are in town (especially during Film Festival season), this is inevitably where some will end up – Goldie Hawn, Cate Blanchett, Sarah Conner, Hardy Krüger Jr and Jette Joop are just a smattering of names the club can drop. It hosts parties too, such as POP Champagne, the Pure White night, Ministry of Sound and an AIDS gala. In 1998 the reins of the club passed into the hands of Nils Heiliger and Frank Schulze-Hagenest, and 90 Grad ('90 degrees') is still burning.

A WALK IN THE PARK

19 Tiergarten

Berlin's 'backyard' spreads over 255 hectares (630 acres) and is the green heart bordering many of the city's central neighbourhoods. Tiergarten (which translates as 'animal garden') was the hunting ground of the Prussian aristocracy in the 16th century and became the largest of the city parks in 1818 when landscape architect Peter Joseph Lenné designed the layout in period English style. Statues began appearing in 1850 and the former processional thoroughfares still traverse the park: five main roads converge at a huge roundabout called the Großer Stern (Big Star), which is crowned at the centre by the Siegessäule (victory column), only one of numerous historical sites within the park's borders. The Schloß Bellevue, home of the federal president, lies to the north and Haus der Kulturen der Welt (House of World Cultures), the former Hall of Congress and now a permanent exhibition site is also situated in the park. Over two-and-a-half hectares (six acres) of lakes and ponds and some 23 kilometres (14 miles) of footpaths run through a range of lawns and overgrown forests. Far from being a prim urban park, Tiergarten comprises wild woods with unruly trees and scattered meadows where family BBQs and bathing take over in the summer months.

PARK LIFE

20 Café am Neuen See

DER TAGESSPIEGEL

Charlottenburg
Wilmersdorf

MOABIT
WESTEND
TIERGARTEN
CHARLOTTENBURG
HALENSEE
WILMERSDORF
Schloß Charlottenburg
Spree
Kaiserin-Augusta-Allee
MIERENDORFFPLATZ
Mierendorffstraße
Nordhauserer Straße
Quedlinburger Straße
Goslarer Ufer
Charlottenburger Ufer
Am Spreebord
Iburger Ufer
Helmholtzstraße
Dovestraße
Franklinstraße
Salzufer
Einsteinufer
Guerickestraße
Cauerstraße
Fraunhoferstraße
Marchstraße
Spandauer Damm
Otto-Suhr-Allee
Kaiser-Friedrich-Straße
RICHARD-WAGNER-PLATZ
Richard-Wagner-Straße
Schustehrus-park
Sophie-Charlotten-Straße
Danckelmannstraße
Nehringstraße
Schloßstraße
Gierkezeile
Wilmersdorfer Straße
Krumme Straße
Zillestraße
Leibnizstraße
Knobelsdorffstraße
Königin-Elisabeth-Straße
Wundtstraße
SOPHIE-CHARLOTTE-PLATZ
BISMARCKSTRASSE
Bismarckstraße
DEUTSCHE OPER
Ernst-Reuter-Platz
ERNST-REUTER-PLATZ
KAISERDAMM
Kaiserdamm
Lietzensee
Schillerstraße
Goethestraße
Pestalozzistraße
Karl-August-Platz
Weimarer Straße
Herderstraße
Schlüterstraße
Knesebeckstraße
Hardenbergstraße
Stein Platz
Carmerstraße
Kantstraße
WILMERSDORFER STRASSE
Savignyplatz
SAVIGNYPLATZ
ZOOLOGISCHER GARTEN
Suarezstraße
Kuno-Fischer-Straße
Dernburgstraße
Herbartstraße
Windscheidstraße
Friedbergstraße
Rönnestraße
CHARLOTTENBURG
Gervinusstraße
Lewishamstraße
Niebuhrstraße
Mommsenstraße
Grolmanstraße
Bleibtreustraße
Uhlandstraße
Fasanenstraße
KURFÜRSTENDAMM
Tauentzienstraße
WITTENBERGPLATZ
UHLANDSTRASSE
Sybelstraße
Giesebrechtstraße
Wielandstraße
Kurfürstendamm
Joachimstaler Straße
Meinekestraße
Rankestraße
Marburger Straße
Nürnberger Straße
Augsburger Straße
Passauer Straße
Ansbacher Straße
AUGSBURGER STRASSE
Lietzenburger Straße
ADENAUERPLATZ
Dahlmannstraße
Roscherstr.
Droysenstraße
Damaschkestr.
Hektorstraße
Nestorstr.
Karlsruher Straße
Joachim-Friedrich-Str.
Katharinenstraße
G.-Wilhelm-Str.
Olivaer Platz
Xantener Straße
Pariser Straße
Duisburger Straße
Schaperstraße
Ludwigkirchstraße
Meierottostraße
Bundesallee
SPICHERNSTRASSE
Düsseldorfer Str.
Zähringerstraße
Wittelsbacherstraße
Württembergische Straße
Sächsische Straße
Emser Straße
Pfalzburger Straße
Konstanzer Straße
Brandenburgische Str.
KONSTANZER STRASSE
Preußen-park
Pommersche Straße
HOHENZOLLERN-PLATZ
Hohenzollerndamm
Westfälische Straße
Paulsborner Straße
Cicerostraße
Albrecht-Achilles-Straße
Eisenzahnstraße
Johann-Georg-Str.
Seesener Straße
Mansfelder Straße
Bielefelder Straße
FEHRBELLINER PLATZ
Trautenaustraße
Güntzelstraße
GÜNTZELSTRASSE
Landhausstraße
Nassauische Straße
Holsteinische Straße
Fechnerstraße
Sigmaringer Straße
Gasteiner Straße
HOHENZOLLERNDAMM
Brienner Straße
Mansfelder Str.
Brandenburgische Straße
Berliner Straße
BLISSESTRASSE
BERLINER STRASSE
Badenschestraße
Approximate scale
1 kilometre
1/2 mile

King Friedrich I gave his wife, Sophie Charlotte, a castle in the village of Lietzow. After her early death he renamed the castle Schloß Charlotte and its surroundings Charlottenburg in her memory. It wasn't long before aristocrats and wealthy bourgeois populated the area, erecting villas and laying out parks. After the industrialization of Charlottenburg and adjacent Wilmersdorf, the area became the residential neighbourhood of choice for the new affluent classes. The atmosphere of a solid upper middle class continues to permeates the area, and offers a foretaste of nearby Grunewald (p. 176), where turn-of-the-century mansions abound in a garden city layout. Around Charlottenburg castle itself is one of the city's museum quarters, with an Egyptian museum and an important collection of Picassos (Sammlung Berggruen), not to mention a pavilion by Berlin architect par excellence, Karl Friedrich Schinkel. The streets around the castle are full of hidden haunts; strollers need only venture off the beaten track to encounter stylish cafés, boutiques and restaurants.

The main drag of Charlottenburg and Wilmersdorf is the posh and elegant Kurfürstendamm, modelled to some degree by Bismarck on the grand boulevards of Hausmann's Paris. (The colloquial name 'Ku'damm' is a good example of how Berliners, in their own way, poke fun at authority: whereas *Kurfürst* is a prince, *Kuh* in German means cow.) It wasn't long after the street's urbanization in 1886 that it spawned residential districts, and in the early 20th century became the lively centre of Berlin's social and cultural life. Between the wars, the area played host to dozens of cinemas and theatres, tea-rooms and cafés that catered to the intellectuals that swarmed there. The Ku'damm was devastated during the Second World War but was soon rebuilt as West Berlin's central artery – the ruin of the Gedächtniskirche (memorial church) at its eastern end is a potent reminder of area's former cultural, physical and artistic turbulence.

Although there remain vestiges of the spirited period before the war, the Ku'damm today is somewhat over represented by tourists. Simply branch off to the south or north on a street like Fasanenstraße, however, and visitors will be rewarded immediately with tranquil tree-lined streets and charming cafés and shops. To the north of Ku'damm, for example, is the delightful square of Savignyplatz, an archetypal western Berlin neighbourhood, where the generation of '68, local students and middle-class inhabitants, mix in high-end boutiques and bars that are filled until the early morning. Charlottenburg is also home to the Technische Universität (TU), a centre of learning that has educated many German thinkers who have achieved international status and whose students ensure that Charlottenburg retains the lively and intellectual animus of former times.

FISHY MYSTERY

1 Jules Verne

Schlüterstraße 61

The name of this charming restaurant is spread about its two rooms in illuminated letters. Not that diners are likely to forget, as there is a quirky dish called 'Ten Thousand Leagues Under the Sea', named for the book that made Jules Verne famous. Red and ivory walls ensure the *Gemütlichkeit* (cosiness), and the little Spanish oak tables squeezed into the space are always full. The portions are huge, hearty and healthy. Buffet lunches are available daily, but à la carte provides substantial dishes designed not to disappoint, with eye-catching names. 'Endless Dream' is linguini with perch and kohlrabi in a herb sauce, 'The Big Apple' is a steak marinated in Calvados with apple and marjoram potatoes.

COLOUR-CODED CLARET

2 Weinrot

132

LITERARY CAFÉ SOCIETY

3 Literaturhaus

Fasanenstraße 23

The rich history of this café-house begins in 1886, when successful iron tradesman Herr Gruson built it and a winter garden annex as a home for his daughter and son-in-law. Created from delicate wrought iron, the house was also used as a showpiece for his firm's work. Gruson's son-in-law, Richard Hilderbrandt, was an explorer and naval captain who travelled to the North Pole and returned a national hero during the reign of Kaiser Wilhelm (Emperor Wilhelm II). The house has had many uses, many related to literature, and has been the 'Literaturhaus' since 1986, providing a home to writers for readings and literary discussion forums. To ensure that the souls and stomachs of the literary set are well nourished there is a lovely café, run by Brigitte and Peter Föste since the early 1990s, with seating that extends into the listed winter garden, one of Berlin's official 'historic gardens'. There is a bookstore on the lower ground level.

CINZANO

ART FROM THE HEART

4 Käthe-Kollwitz-Museum

Fasanenstraße 24

One of the central figures of German Realism and one of the greatest graphic artists of the century, Käthe Kollwitz is best remembered for her compassionate portrayals of the poor in Berlin during the first half of the 20th century. Married to a doctor and a socialist, she witnessed first-hand the travails of the lower classes, which she dispassionately yet sensitively depicted in lithographs, woodcuts, etchings, charcoal drawings and sculpture, believing that perhaps her art could bring about social change. This private house-museum, founded in 1986 by collector Hans Pels-Leusden in a grand private residence next door to the Literaturhaus, shows a permanent collection of some two hundred of Kollwitz's drawings and graphic works, a number of which are well known and deeply moving.

SUITS TO SUIT

5 Patrick Hellmann

Fasanenstraße 28 & 29

Sentences containing the phrases 'a New York minute', 'Time is money' and 'Moscow is booming' were uttered by Patrick Hellmann's staff in a period of less than twenty Berlin minutes and give a taste of the buzzy ambience that the American designer, who moved to Berlin over twenty years ago, has created in his atelier. Son of a German tailor, Hellmann grew up in Cincinnati, Ohio, and learnt tailoring techniques from a young age. Hellmann's suit empire began with one store in 1980, which has expanded to three in Berlin and three in Moscow; he developed a women's line in 1998 and boys' clothes in 2001. Presenting two collections a year, couture and prêt-à-porter, he is known for an instantly recognizable smart but comfortable pin-stripe suit. He is extending his talents into home ware, with fabric photo frames, lamps and furniture (a chair upholstered in pin-stripe), all bearing the Hellmann touch.

SOMETHING SPECIAL

6 Galerie Bremer

A BOTTLE OF RUM

7 RumTrader

Fasanenstraße 40

'The New York Fire Department does not allow more than 150 people in the Establishment' reads a prominent sign on the wall near the entrance of RumTrader. The irony is that the entire room measures not much more than 100 square feet (ten square metres) and could seat no more than a dozen people before it became unbearably overcrowded. Yet these constraints have done little to diminish the bar's raging popularity since it was opened in 1975 by Hans Schrooder, who once ran the bar at the original Adlon Hotel. After 27 years he passed it on to Gregor Schöll, conception consultant for the Paris Bar (p. 131), who has been at the helm since 2001. Over 150 types of rum are in stock, and small tastings are held to sample rarer varieties. Schöll has two special events a year on the premises: the RumTrader Christmas Party is a charity event for the Salvation Army, and the late British Queen Mother's birthday on 4 August is also celebrated. One of his favourite rum cocktails was named in her honour, and he has a letter from Buckingham Palace acknowledging the drink.

MEDITERRANEAN ORGANIC

8 Hotel Bleibtreu

Bleibtreustraße 31

The idea behind Germany's first boutique hotel was a Mediterranean theme. Hotel Bleibtreu was the third Berlin hotel creation of Roman Skoblo, who followed his first, The Savoy, with the Berliner Hof; his fourth and latest is Ku'Damm 101 (p. 124). The new hotel building was designed by Herbert Jakob Weinand, but the interior's warm blue tones infused with red were chosen by Zurich-based Kreativbüro Kessler + Kessler, whose intention was to incorporate Weinand's unique design to create a southern European energy. The hotel is set back from the street, fronted by a flower shop that specializes in international rose imports and an espresso bar that backs on to a gourmet restaurant. A long mosaic-tiled table shadowed by a chestnut tree is the focus of the inner courtyard and a popular candlelit summer evening drinking destination. Sixty rooms with an organic ethos (apples instead of chocolates on your pillow) and a wellness spa complete the Bleibtreu experience.

CREAMING DECADENCE

9 Kaufhaus Schrill

Bleibtreustraße 46

This old-school shop is a Berlin oddity. Berliner Irene Schweitzer's eye for high-class farce is played out in the store, which she opened in 1981. 'This city was grey in the early 1980s,' she remembers, 'and I wanted to throw some colour around.' She had been living in London and Florence and travelled to New York and Hong Kong looking for retro objects to sell back home. Among the eclectic items her shop has carried are sunglasses from the 1950s onwards, costume jewelry, a rainbow of gloves, 1920s hats and a jacket designed by a costumier who used to dress Elvis Presley. 'I am also famous for "conversation ties",' she proudly explains, referring to the ties popular in the 1980s printed to look like keyboards or fish. There is something for everyone (going to a fancy dress party) at Kaufhaus Schrill. 'I am also hot on extreme wigs,' Schweitze says.

BAUHAUS IN THE HOUSE

10 Art + Industry

Bleibtreustraße 40

Since 1987 Art + Industry has been collecting vintage furniture to restore, sell or rent, developing an exclusive selection of tubular-steel furniture selected from the 1930s to 1950s and other classics from the 1950s to 1980s. Anything that cannot fit in the shop is housed in the 3,200-square-foot (300-square-metre) factory outlet on nearby Wilmersdorfer Straße. To visit either showroom is akin to taking a walk around a design museum, with the added benefit of being able to sit on the Bauhaus chairs available for purchase. Pieces by Marianne Brandt, Christian Dell, Wilhelm Wagenfeld and Marcel Breuer are frequently in the store, as is an extensive Bauhaus collection, glassware from the Czech Republic and Italian Murano glass. Antique fans and watches, Bakelite jewelry and Scandinavian silver complete the range of often museum-quality small pieces.

WINE SPECIALIST

11 Klemkes Wein- und Spezialitäteneck

Mommsenstraße 9

When Werner Klemkes sold luxury leather goods, he and his suppliers often enjoyed drinking wine. What started as a hobby developed into a lifestyle as he traded in his Cartier and Hermès for Cabernet and Merlot to set up a shop in Berlin twenty years ago. Klemkes travels regularly around Europe, tasting wines and learning the history of vineyards to buy wines two to three years in advance. His vast selection is stored on wooden shelves and sold alongside plates of home-made local fare prepared by his wife, Elfi. There is nowhere to sit but regulars are happy to eat standing. Klemkes is a veritable encyclopedia when it comes to wine: 'I am in my seventies,' he says, 'and I know wine. I share a bottle a day with Elfi and that means we are sure of what we sell and what we like.'

SMOKIN'

12 Zigarren Herzog

Ludwigkirchplatz 1

Dr Maximilian Herzog's raison d'être is teaching people how to smoke cigars. With this mission he arrived in Berlin in the late 1990s and established a shop that can only be described as an altar to the art of cigar-smoking. His reputation and knowledge have led to him moonlighting as the man behind the humidor and cigar bar at the Savoy Hotel's Times Bar, whose leather sofas and parquet flooring create a warm ambience. Zigarren Herzog, on the leafy Ludwigkirchplatz, a quiet residential square in a neighbourhood where cigar-smoking types abound, not far away, encompasses several rooms and a walk-in humidor. Herzog takes delight in educating his customers and explaining the rituals and history of cigar smoking, and organizing events, usually alongside a port tasting or demonstration of hand-rolling cigars.

NEW BERLIN NOW

13 Leibniz Kolonnaden

Between Leibnizstraße and Wielandstraße

Against the traditional architecture of Charlottenburg, the stark modernity of Leibniz Kolonnaden is striking. The recently completed arcade was named in honour of the philosopher-mathematician who developed calculus, and it has been hailed as a new way of life for Berliners. To live, shop, work and eat – the mixed-use colonnade was designed to accommodate the upwardly mobile in loft-style upper-story spaces, with offices, shops and restaurants lining the ground level. The clean, rigid lines of the structure have proved a popular destination, with people dining, playing and relaxing there all year round. Enoiteca Il Calice is the restaurant of choice for foodies, and young families will enjoy the water fountains that spring straight from the ground when the weather is warm.

HAT FASHION

14 Chapeaux

Bleibtreustraße 51

In 1994 Andrea Curti completed her training with milliner Gunter Baumbach and began to sell hats in a space she shared with Fiebelkorn and Kuckuck (p. 98) before opening her own store across the street in 1999. A dark wooden floor, dark blue walls and a deep purple crushed-velvet sofa transform her space into a prismatic black hole with illuminated wall areas displaying her vast range of hats. Curti believes that hats make people 'look better and more individual. In summer I design for shade and protection and in winter for warmth, but all year round I want them to be funky and personality-enhancing.' 'Chapeaux' is also a colloquialism for 'Ah, nice!', the reaction Curti would like to elicit from her customers whenever and wherever they don her creations. Alongside everyday hats for men and women are sculptural feather affairs in lime green and mustard, which have inspired her recent foray into matching bags.

LATIN INFLUENCE

15 Rio

Bleibtreustraße 52

Originally from Lübeck, Barbara Kranz celebrated twenty years of jewelry design in Berlin in 2004. Kranz may not have been to Rio, but her work is full of colour and spice. 'For me, Rio is a flowing river,' Kranz says. 'There is movement and colour and music and post-robbery money.' Aware that some women like to be noticed, she mixes vintage stones – old glass atmospheric beads, for example – with decorative acrylic beads, which take dye well and allow designers to experiment with dynamic colour schemes that scream, 'See me, touch me, love me, want me!' Kranz's metalwork too is unique, moulding copper and silver and brass to enhance the tones of the gems.

STAR IN THE ASCENDANT

16 Lubitsch

REVENGE OF THE WOMAN

17 Revanche de la Femme

Uhlandstraße 50

Six metal supports give shape to each of the corsets that Shimon Troianovski and Elena Krebs produce under their racily titled label, Revanche de la Femme. So successful was their first store, which opened in 1999, that it was followed by a second on the Ku'damm in 2003. The Russian-German partnership began when Krebs returned to Berlin after studying fashion in Kiev. Their corsets are indisputably beautiful, and the exquisite ability with which the pieces 'hold you in' have garnered customers from teenagers to grandmothers. The shop features a dizzying array of styles, colours and fabrics, from front- and back-fastening corsets, each with their own style; the Exclusive line incorporates corsets into dresses and tops.

DESIGNER SUPERSTORE

18 Stilwerk

Kantstraße 17

Fifty-nine outlets for 500 brands occupying more than 19,000 square metres (200,000 square feet) spread over five floors – these are the impressive vital statistics of the Stilwerk furniture and design complex. An idea born in Hamburg to investor Bernhard Garbe, Stilwerk houses the best international contemporary design under one roof. All the usual suspects are present and accounted for: Kartell (chairs), Alessi (Italian kitchen accessories), Niessing (German contemporary jewelry design), Bang & Olufsen (high-tech hi-fi), Ligne Roset (Italian sofas), Bulthaup (kitchens) and even Bechstein (pianos). Many of these familiar names are synonymous with quality and style and are available elsewhere, so for those seeking more indigenous talent, try the Handwerk + Design Platform on the fourth level. Here newcomers display aquariums, bean-bags and other novel and functional decorative ideas – you might just discover one of tomorrow's stars.

THE LINK

19 Neues Kranzler Eck

Between Kurfürstendamm and Kantstraße

Proximity to Zoologischer Bahnhof and the relocation of posh shopping to Friedrichstraße from former West Berlin throughout the 1990s left the eastern ends of Ku'damm and Kantstraße somewhat soulless. As a revitalization initiative, architect Helmut Jahn (see also p. 38) designed a passageway that links the thoroughfares' dead-ends with one shiny, bright arcade. Stark, glass buildings now glow with white neon light, turning night to day in a paved row of fashion and interior boutiques, animating the area between the Theater des Westens (known for its musicals), the Delphi Cinema (famous for its own 1920s architecture and grand interior), the Savoy Hotel and British high-tech architect Nicholas Grimshaw's interstellar Stock Exchange. Look out for Württemberger, a specialist wine shop selling bottles from southwest Germany.

TWO IN ONE

20 Fiebelkorn and Kuckuck

Bleibtreustraße 4

Two women. Two designers. Two styles. Two sets of clientele. One space. This is the formula that is Fiebelkorn and Kuckuck. 'Nanna and I simply share a shop,' explains Friederike Fiebelkorn. 'Our styles are so different that it is rare for us ever to have one customer who feels committed to both of us.' This is because Fiebelkorn designs bridal dresses and Kuckuck glamorous evening wear. The bridal line tends toward the traditional, but Fiebelkorn is quick to point out that this is because of the preferences of Berlin women rather than her own imagination. Kuckuck makes her own pleats and then sculpts dresses using Italian fabrics and antique saris. They both love the effect of draping and abhor black. 'There is too much of that safe colour in this city,' comments Fiebelkorn. 'We prefer to play with tones.'

WHY, CUE THE STYLE

21 Q!

120

ART BOOK

22 Galerie 2000

Knesebeckstraße 56–58

Wolfgang Chrobot has created an environment that is just what an art bookshop should be: shelf upon shelf of volumes that run from floor to ceiling, surrounding great display tables groaning under the weight of books. 'There is no room for posters or exhibitions on my walls,' Chrobot admits. Since he opened his specialist art bookstore in 1970 he has amassed over 35,000 titles: 'I am a bookseller's dream,' he says, a claim verified by Germany's famous book dealer Walter König, who thinks that Galerie 2000 is the best bookstore in the land. 'I feel the same way about him,' says Chrobot. Art, architecture, photography and design books crowd into Galerie 2000 along with an impressive exhibition catalogue collection and books on tribal African, Asian and South American art.

LIFE IS A CABARET

23 Bar Jeder Vernunft

Schaper Straße 24

Familiar names and those who hope to become so happily share the stage at this mini-cabaret restaurant, founded by Holger Klotzbach in 1992 in an old Art Nouveau circus tent (complete with red-velvet–lined boxes and sparkling mirrors). The stage is set every night for a ringmaster to take the performers through their paces to the delight of spectators who can feast on food provided by Florian (p. 138) while they watch the show unfold. Otto Sander, Max Raabe and Ute Lemper have trodden these boards, as well as drag queen Georgette Dee and comedian Jockel Tschiersch. The shows change, but the line-up is usually a twist on musical, comedy, political satire, performance and wit.

ORGIASTIC FOOD FEST

24 KaDeWe

169

ZEN WINTER GARDEN

25 Hotel Brandenburger Hof

122

PHOTO ICON

26 Museum für Fotografie

Jebensstraße 2

Following his tragic recent death in a car accident, it was perhaps no surprise that fashion photographer and native Berliner Helmut Newton should have a museum dedicated to his prolific body of work, which forms part of this new museum for photography. Intended as a centre for passionate photographers to learn and show, Newton donated a large collection to the city, which is housed in an old art library located down an odd alleyway behind the Zoologischer Bahnhof, an area where the homeless, prostitutes and drug users are more prevalent than art-luvvies. And yet Newton never shied away from the seedy underbelly, as many of his photographs demonstrate. His career spanned people and situations from all walks of life, from the famous to the derelict.

OOH-LA-LA

27 Paris Bar

131

FRIEDERIKE
IEBELKORN
FIEBELKORN
TOFFE
INDISCHE SEIDEN
FRANZÖSISCHE SP
ITALIENISCHE STC
Bar
eder

DIE ADRIA
KATHARINENKLOSTER
AUF DEM SINAI
FÈS
Art et Architectures Berbères du Maroc
CAIRO
Alger
à l'époque ottomane
Piazza San Carlo a Torino
SIZILIEN
Mythos, Kunst und Kultur
Putz
und
Stuck
ASMARA
Byzantium
Rediscovered
CAFÉ
SAVIGNY

HOMAGE TO AUSTRIA

28 Ottenthal

SOUL FOOD SECRET

29 Florian

138

JE T'AIME

30 Gainsbourg

BOXING RING

31 Diener Tattersall

WHAT'S IN A NAME

32 Weinrestaurant Risachér

Savignyplatz 11

Savignyplatz is a bustling square where the local chattering classes head for when they are feeling peckish. Yet the Weinrestaurant Risachér is an oasis among the breakfast cafés and bars. Over twenty years ago owner and namesake Yves Risachér started serving his Alsatian French–German cuisine and its long existence is proof enough of its popularity. The underlying theme is that tradition and classic cooking will outlast trends, and this is also apparent in the décor of the restaurant. Simple primary colours on the walls contrast with a predominant use of wood that is reminiscent of quaint rural German B&Bs. The boeuf bourguignon and mousse au chocolat are world class.

COSY CUBBY

33 Café Savigny

Grolmanstraße 53

This low-key local café has been serving huge platters of comfort food to its customers since 1981. It is the domain of Heidi Schöfa, who has created a homey feel in the two-room space with faux-Roman friezes on the walls, painted in typically Prussian hues, an old-fashioned chandelier and round tables. Daily newspapers in four languages are background reading for the changing menu, which features such favourites as gnocchi and German pasta ravioli stuffed with meat and accompanied by potatoes. Tea-time is catered for in the vast selection of cakes, coffees and chocolates. A local favourite, it retains its café atmosphere long into the evening.

UNDERNEATH THE ARCHES

34 Bücherbogen

Savignyplatz, Bogen 593

Berliner Gerhard Spangenberg is an architect and owner of the Bücherbogen chain of design and architecture bookshops, which has grown to six outlets in the city. He and his wife, Ruthild, opened this, the first and largest store, over twenty years ago in a derelict space under three railway arches (*Bücherbogen* means 'book arch') off Savignyplatz. The design of the interiors is appropriate for the extensive range of architecture, design, graphic design, theory, art and photography volumes that attract professionals, students and browsers. Readings and launches of new editions are regularly held here.

ARCHITECTURAL OVERVIEW

35 Galerie Aedes

Savignyplatz, Bogen 600–1

The ambition of Galerie Aedes is 'to clarify that architecture is not merely an isolated method of construction but that it operates as a political, cultural and communal process as well'. After almost a quarter century, few in the international architecture circles would disagree that the gallery has achieved its mission through Kristin Feireiss, who with Hans-Jürgen Commerell founded the gallery in 1980. A second, non-profit space in the Hackesche Höfe was opened more recently. Every year the gallery presents eighteen to twenty exhibitions by renowned and experimental architects, including over the years such luminaries as Daniel Libeskind, Frank Gehry, Rem Koolhaas, Zaha Hadid, MVRDV and Tadao Ando. In 2001 Feireiss was awarded the Cross of Order of Merit of the Federal Republic of Germany for her contribution to architecture.

CHOCOLATE LOVE STORY

36 Melanie

-August-Platz
Universum
Lounge

OFF TO MARKET

37 Karl-August-Platz

• Biscotti, Pestalozzistraße 88

Having a dinner party and want to get the freshest organic produce? The local market is where local culinary enthusiasts come to pick out and pick up native cheeses, breads, fruit and vegetables from an impressive selection. The delectable bakery stalls entice passers-by with scents of warm *Brötchen*, plus a variety of *Roggen-*, *Weizen-* and *Mischbrot*. Small market stalls tucked under white canvas canopies are set out around the Evangelische Trinitatis-Kirche like a string of pearls around the neck of a grande dame. Set in the quintessentially residential backyard of Charlottenburg, the square has its own charm relatively untouched by tourists. Several coffee-houses overlook the market bustle, the pick of the bunch being Biscotti for that after-shop consideration of what you've bought and what you're going to cook with it over a cappuccino and torte.

UNIVERSAL EXPERIENCE

38 Universum Lounge

Kurfürstendamm 153

Part of a complex originally designed by master Expressionist architect Erich Mendelsohn, which includes a theatre and health-conscious café, this space-age lounge bar is the design product of hot Berlin architecture duo Alexander Plajer and Werner Franz (see also p. 28), who created an futuristic décor with enigmatic photographs illuminated by light boxes.

DANCE ELECTRIC

39 Mendelsohn Complex

Kurfürstendamm 153

Also included in Mendelsohn's complex are the Schaubühne am Lehniner Platz, once one of the most important German-speaking theatres and still known for its avant-garde performances. Today it is home to a new set of choreographers and directors headed by Sascha Waltz and Thomas Ostermeier (he brought Mark Ravenhill's *Shopping and Fucking* to the Berlin boards). With a redesigned theatre by Jürgen Sawade and a rough concrete interior with free-standing chairs, the space has an impromptu feel that is balanced by state-of-the-art hydraulic stage machinery.

BLOW YOUR MIND SKY HIGH

40 Propeller Island City Lodge

118

MINIMALIST UNDERSTATEMENT

41 Ku'Damm 101

124

LAKE DISTRICT

42 Engelbecken

Witzlebenstraße 31

Situated beside the Lietzensee lake, Engelbecken boasts that rare quality in an urban restaurant in which customers feel as though they are in the country, especially in the summer, when tables are dragged out onto the street corner to overlook the azure calm of this inner-city lake. German–Austrian cuisine heightens the illusion of the south, and Engelbecken is justly proud of its *Braten* (roasts) and Schnitzel. The name Engelbecken refers to its former location near its namesake river in Kreuzberg, where it was a successful institution eaterie. Indoors, a marvellously simple décor of stark white walls with green linoleum floor, dark-brown tables and chairs, give the traditional menu a modern contrast. After dinner lakeside strolls are a perfect digestif.

OLD PERFECTIONIST

43 Alt-Luxemburg

135

TOWN PALACE

44 Schloß Charlottenburg

Spandauer Damm 20–24

Built as a summer residence for Queen Sophie-Charlotte by her husband, King Friedrich I, the oldest standing Prussian palace dates back to 1695, though wings were added in the 18th and 19th centuries, themselves fine examples of period architecture and art. The Neue Flügel (New Wing) was built by Knobeldorff and the Neue Pavillon (New Pavilion) by Karl Friedrich Schinkel in 1824. On the castle grounds are the Stüler Bau Pavilion, which houses the impressive Sammlung Berggruen, the bequest of Heinz Berggruen, who left Berlin for the United States in 1933 but donated 69 Picassos and works by Cézanne, van Gogh, Klee and Giacometti for the collection. All the buildings are set in landscaped grounds, originally laid out in 1697 and today a pleasing setting for jogging locals and dog walkers all year round.

Style Traveller

sleep • eat • drink
shop • retreat

sleep

The cultural richness of Berlin is mirrored directly in the extreme range of choice of the guest accommodation it offers. From gleaming towers of high-tech splendour to wild bohemian bolt-holes, from the hotel as *Gesamtkunstwerk* to hotel as industrial design object, there is something for every taste in the city's lodgings. A tribute to the creative efflorescence Berlin has enjoyed since reunification, art is a consistent theme in many of these hotels – whether hung on the walls or in the form of the rooms themselves.

HONEYMOON HOTEL

14 Honigmond Garden Hotel

10 Invalidenstraße 112

Rooms from €160

Dr Carl Loyal was painting the walls of his first hotel when the Beatles 1963 'Honeymoon Song' was aired on the radio. His literal translation became the name of the hotel he acquired to provide affordable accommodation for young people. Before 1989, the restaurant on the corner of Borsigstraße and Tieckstraße had been popular with opposition DDR politicians and as a result was shut down by the Stasi for reasons of 'overcrowding', but in 1999 Loyal reopened it, along with the hotel. After discovering a defunct building with a wild inner garden on nearby Invalidenstraße in 2000, he opened his second establishment, the Honigmond Garden Hotel. Twenty rooms, six garden cabins and three suites all designed and furnished by Loyal provide comfort with a genuine feel of home. Loyal believes in an honesty system, so there is a piggy bank for guests to pay the minimal charge for wine or hot drinks from the mini-bar in the communal lounge. He lives on the premises, and his love of gardening, design and art pervades the building. Frogs and fish inhabit a garden pond crossed by a Japanese-style bridge. Loyal has clearly hit on a winning formula: 'Some guests like it here so much they never leave the hotel for the duration of their Berlin stay. They invite their friends over and hang out in the garden instead.'

ART HOUSE HOTEL

14 **Luise: Hotel + Künstlerheim**

58 Luisenstraße 19

Rooms from €130

Former art-gallery owner Christian Bree and music venue manager Mike Buller joined forces in 1995 to open a hotel in a derelict building in former East Berlin that was so decrepit there was little interest in renovating it. Budgetary constraints forced the pair to rely on friends and contacts, so between 1995 and 1998 they opened the rooms as blank canvases to artist friends. An ambitious renovation in 1998 by architect Rainer Seiferth meant the Luise could officially reopen in 1999 as the 47-room establishment it is today. 'No two rooms are the same and each is done by a different artist,' explains Bree. The artists range from the well known to the art student. 'We regularly approach the Universität der Künste (Art Academy) in Berlin, looking for design candidates for the third-floor rooms. If we choose a student then we also provide him with a budget and 5% of the income of that room until we change it again.' Most of the rooms have been created by established artists, and staying in them is like a lesson in contemporary art: Thomas Baumgärtel celebrated his forty-third birthday and twenty years of banana art in 2003. The so-called Banana Sprayer is the man behind the yellow bananas painted on the exterior of reputable Berlin galleries. Once illegal (he was arrested for graffiti), they are now coveted as the mark of a quality contemporary gallery. His Royal Suite at the Luise is easily identifiable for its Baumgärtel-sprayed walls with signature bananas. A room designed by sculptor Jochen Schmiddem, who was the set designer for Steven Spielberg's *Minority Report*, features a provocative, confusing, hanging sculpture. Elvira Bach has been creating for some 40 years and printed self-portraits on her walls. The Luise's appeal lies in the high art of its rooms, each a beguiling, finished art work reflecting the history and ideas of its creator – and the creativity of Berlin.

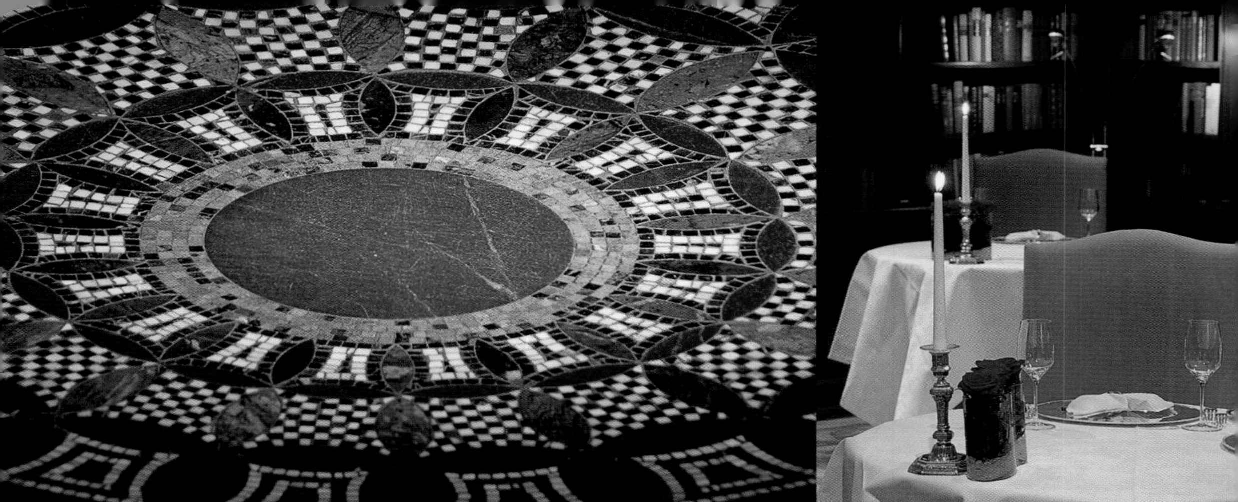

HOTEL LORE

14

Hotel Adlon Kempinski

68 Unter den Linden 77

Rooms from €370

Hotel Adlon's story is the stuff of legend. At its inauguration on 23 October 1907, Emperor Wilhelm II decreed that no guest be allowed to enter the hotel before him and paid a handsome annual retainer of 150,000 Deutschmarks to secure his needs there. Hotel Adlon soon became the unofficial guesthouse for diplomats and a pied-à-terre for the local aristocracy. Its services – hot running water, gas, electricity and a cooling and refrigeration system – marked it as the ultimate in luxury at the time, which attracted more famous guests, including Albert Einstein, Charlie Chaplin and Greta Garbo, who whispered, 'I want to be alone' while there filming *Grand Hotel*, which was based on the Hotel Adlon. In 1921 founder Lorenz Adlon's son Louis took over the management and in time it was referred to as Berlin's 'Little Switzerland' as, despite the disturbances of political regimes, it managed to maintain a neutral international ambience. Hitler once dined there. It was used as a hospital during the Second World War, during which it went untouched until the night of 2 May 1945, when an internal fire started and all but one wing was razed to the ground. The hotel's traditions lived on in that surviving wing.

It was Communism that marked the Adlon's downfall. The hotel represented capitalist decadence at its most extreme, so the Communist regime converted it into a hostel for apprentices, and in 1984 the last remaining wing was destroyed to make way for a new residential complex. When the Wall fell on 9 November 1989, however, rebuilding was a sign of optimistic times, and in August 1997 the reborn hotel was declared open by Federal President Roman Herzog. So famous is the hotel that books have paid tribute to it as well as a movie, *The Heyday of Hotel Adlon*, by Percy Adlon, who also directed *Baghdad Café*. Managing Director Jean K. van Daalen is currently President of the Hotel and Restaurant Association of Berlin. Both George Bushes, the Dalai Lama and Mikhail Gorbachev have been guests of the hotel, which boasts 336 rooms, two restaurants, a spa, two winter gardens, conference facilities and two presidential suites.

LIGHT AND SPACE

14 **Dorint am Gendarmenmarkt**

63 Charlottenstraße 50–52

Rooms from €240

Harald Klein and Bert Haller are behind the high-concept look at this Dorint Hotel. The challenge for the interior design duo from Mönchengladbach was to invent a contemporary 'design hotel' interior on what must be Berlin's most stunning baroque square. The cobbled Gendarmenmarkt is the site of two cathedrals, the Französischer Dom (French Cathedral, which now houses the Hugenottenmusuem) and the Deutscher Dom (German Cathedral), both built by Carl von Gontard for Friedrich II during the 1780s, as copies of the Santa Maria in Montesanto and the Santa Maria dei Miracoli in Rome. The views from the Dorint rooms' windows on to the square are magnificent. Under the management of Tini Countess Rothkirch, Klein and Haller experimented with lighting effects to create an ambience that would feel cool and inviting, while respecting the rich architectural environs. The Delphinium conference room, for example, is illuminated with glowing floor tiles and sleek, slimline chandeliers, creating a futuristic aesthetic. All 92 rooms and suites have sliding glass walls, which allow for adjustment of space and light in the marble-floored bathrooms. The two top floors have been dedicated to physical wellbeing and house a quirky gym (high-tech equipment sits next to a dusty leather sofa on dark wooden floors) and a wellness spa on a decked balcony. The effects of sauna, steam room and plunge-pool are enhanced by a colour-therapy relaxation area, which boasts reclining chairs, each equipped with a personal stereo.

SHOWER
CAP
ADA GmbH
D-77677 Kehl

URBAN SANCTUARY

14 **Madison**

72 Potsdamer Straße 3

Rooms from €120

An oasis of Zen-inspired calm discreetly located in the heart of the *Matrix*-esque architecture of Potsdamer Platz is the personal vision of Lutz Hesse and Christian Andresen. After cutting their teeth in the hotel industries of Germany, Switzerland and California, the two colleagues decided to go it alone and in 1997 opened the Madison Suites on Friederichstraße. The success of the quietly conservative business apartments allowed the duo to take a more ambitious step in the direction of a design hotel, and in 1999 Madison Potsdamer Platz became their second city-centre establishment. Andresen oversees the business side of the partnership, and Hesse is responsible for creating the aesthetic experience. 'For me it is all about the details,' he explains. 'This hotel is an expression of my vision and that is evolving all the time. What you see at the Madison is a work in progress.' And quite a work it is: a first-floor lounge bar called Qiu (p. 157); Facil (p. 140), their Michelin-starred restaurant on the fifth floor with a garden terrace; a wellness spa on the roof boasting incredible views across Berlin's post-modern skyline of new development, thrusting crane action and the changing light moods of the Sony Centre across the street. Hesse takes great pleasure in his job, and this feeling of enjoyment pervades the hotel and staff attitudes. Twice weekly he rises at 4.00 in the morning to buy flowers directly from the market and makes all the floral displays himself. Black-and-white prints by Ellen Auerbach adorn the walls of 166 suites, and each room is packed with state-of-the-art DVD player and and plasma screens. It is all in keeping with the glass façade of the eleven-storey building designed by Lauber & Wöhr Architecture, mixing purist Asian ideology in a clean-lined, clean-living design space where the weary are guaranteed regeneration.

BLOW YOUR MIND SKY HIGH

88 **Propeller Island City Lodge**

 Albrecht-Achilles-Straße 58

Rooms from €80

It was in 1986 that the initial concept of Propeller Island took hold in the public consciousness. Native Berliner Lars Stroschen registered it as an umbrella name to cover the variety of music, art, electronic and text-based projects that were making him a notorious personality on the city's edgy art scene. Music composition for live dance and art projects, and CD releases filled his time until 1993, when Propeller Island was realized as a physical manifestation in Stroschen's City Lodge. His dream was to create a living piece of art that could be inhabited. An evolving canvas of ideas has expanded to cover three floors and some 45 rooms, each unique and many the work of Stroschen. Guests are encouraged to choose their rooms by viewing Propeller Island's website, where each is featured with a mini-description. The dazzling choice is inspiring, a tangible vision unfolding in slide-show format: Orange features a citrus colour scheme that aims to impart a sunny state on those who stay here, Forest displays one hundred Nordic runes in a chromatic reflection, which become dancing lights at dawn, and Space Cube is all blue light and gadgets. But some of the rooms are intended for those seeking a more challenging overnight experience: the Freedom room is designed ironically to resemble a Dalí-esque version of a prison cell (complete with toilet in room and an escape hole in the wall) and an upside-down room has furniture on the ceiling. As a living art project some rooms are dismantled and replaced by new ideas, and ensuring that no sense is left untouched, Stroschen composes and programmes the interior music.

WHY, CUE THE STYLE

88 **Q!**

21 Knesebeckstraße 67

Rooms from €150

Open since Spring 2004, Q! is the brainchild of Wolfgang Loock, who commissioned Berlin and Los Angeles based architects Graft to design a building that explored space and the formulaic use of structure in an innovative and practical way. The result is a high-design interior whose multifaceted surfaces will help redefine the hotel room: walls are curved to double as pieces of furniture; baths and beds are inherently part of each room's architecture. Thomas Willemeit, Lars Krückeberg and Wolfram Putz, who had cooperated with actor Brad Pitt on a studio and guest house for him, wanted to create a sense of curvaceous comfort in their cocoon-rooms.

The colours of Q! suit Berlin; warm tones of red cover the walls and floors of the bar area and are exotically complimented by imitation ostrich leather and balanced by slate and dark wood. Loock took the concept of the private member's bar so popular in London and New York, and reproduced it in Q!'s own watering hole. He imported Ben Reed, an ex-manager of London's successfully select Met Bar (part of the Metropolitan Hotel) to consult and concoct the cocktail menu and drinks list. Food is available, and a rotation of DJs provide the aural back-drop. Underneath the rooms and party central is a subterranean wellness centre. The Sandraum's unique selling point is hot sand floors with a room-temperature permanently set to body-temperature, which promises to boost the immune system of those who spend time there. Add the Japanese washing zone, which doubles as hammam, and Q! pushes the limits of the design hotel to new boundaries.

ZEN WINTER GARDEN

88 **Hotel Brandenburger Hof**

25 Eislebener Straße 14
Rooms from €250

A grand double-door façade hides the entrance, concealing the building's former life as an apartment block and the intimate hotel within. Located on a leafy quiet residential street, Hotel Brandenburger Hof was transformed in 1991 into one of the most discreet hotels in the city, with a number of pleasant surprises within. Owner Daniela Sauter employed her architect-brother Peter Sauter to revamp the former flats, which become an 82-room hotel with a formal gourmet restaurant, Die Quadriga, piano bar, library and a wellness spa. Working with Japanese architect Kenji Tsuchiya, Sauter achieved a sophisticated fusion of modern European design enhanced by traditional Eastern colours and style. One of the hotel's unexpected delights is the Zen-inspired Wintergarten, with its stone floor punctuated by lemon trees, water pools and free-flying finches, and an ikebana master is responsible for the hotel's daily flower arrangements. The Wintergarten is also the breakfast room, offering a veritable feast of cooked and fresh foods and an irresistible *Birchermuesli*, and acts as the lounge leading into the Michelin-starred restaurant.

Die Quadriga is the domain of Wolfgang Nagler, who since 2000 has been a member of the circle of eight master head chefs of Berlin. He serves classic French cuisine on KPM (p. 36) porcelain with Robbe and Berking cutlery, in a cherry-wood wall-panelled room, to guests seated on matching wooden chairs based on a 1904 Frank Lloyd Wright design. In fact, design classics are littered throughout the hotel: Le Corbusier and Mies van der Rohe chairs, Wagenfeld lamps in the rooms and limited-edition prints by Ernst Fuchs, Bruno Bruni and Claude Gaveau on the walls. In the Brandenburger Hof, the Sauters have achieved a rare state of cultural harmony that is at once peaceful and invigorating.

MINIMALIST UNDERSTATEMENT

88 Ku'Damm 101

41 Kurfürstendamm 101
Rooms from €120

Minimalism is the visual theme at Ku'Damm 101: even its name is no more than the street address. The whole building was designed a decade ago by Eyl, Weitz, Würmle & Partner and sat vacant while Roman Skoblo debated his intentions. Finally committing to the hotel project, he asked Kessler + Kessler, the husband-and-wife design partnership who have been responsible for the aesthetic of all four of Skoblo's hotels in Berlin (Savoy, Bleibtreu, p. 93, and Berliner Hof), to take on the interiors. In keeping with a city-wide theme, Franziska Kessler began with a single signature base colour – here grey, in pale and dark shades – subscribing to the theory of Swiss architect Le Corbusier that harmony in a building's colour tones promotes the well-being and happiness of those who reside there. Light, creamy-grey rubber floors and darker walls are teamed with storm-coloured support pillars in the communal areas. Extending this idea, Kessler gave each of the seven floors its own palette, all provided by kt.COLOR, the Swiss firm who are licensed to manufacture Le Corbusier's original pigments. Their walls have been kept art-free but each room boasts an Arne Jacobsen Series 7 chair and furniture by young German designers. Munich's Lemongras Design Studio provided the wardrobes and novelty tables, which have extendable, manoeuvrable lap-top flaps. The breakfast and conference rooms on the seventh floor offer an inspiring vista over the city, while the sinuous lime-green lounge bar downstairs heats up at night.

eat

Like all great cosmopolises, Berlin offers world-class dining experiences and off-beat ethnic eateries, but this is to underappreciate German cuisine, honed through centuries of tradition and more recently influenced by global trends. The eclectic selection here reflects a variety of traditional, regional and modern German cooking, alongside restaurants with an Eastern European flavour, international hot spots and a handful of timeless classics. For the quintessence of Berlin eating – and Berliners' overwhelmingly favourite meal – look out for *Frühstück* (breakfast), usually served all day long throughout the capital.

WINE GUY

WeinGuy

Luisenstraße 19

Before opening WeinGuy, Hartmut Guy had already established a reputation with Gasthaus am Weiner (a theatre restaurant) in Freudenberg and a large gourmet French restaurant near the Gendarmenmarkt. WeinGuy – as the name suggests – is a speciality wine restaurant, serving a predominantly German fare. For the setting Guy cleverly appropriated a disused space under railway tracks to create a curved, brick-lined environment extending through two arches, that is at once cosy and reminiscent of medieval times. The space changes as morning guests from the adjacent Hotel Luise (p. 110) taking breakfast give way to the lunch crowd; from the afternoon the wine emporium stays open until dinner guests come to choose a bottle to accompany their meal. There is an astonishing selection of over 1,500 wines, 60 of which are available by the glass, and sommelier Mike Talabudzinow is on hand to explain them all. Hard-core regulars rent space in Guy's temperature-controlled wine cabinets.

HISTORY IN THE MAKING

58 **Café Adler**

2 Friedrichstraße 206

Angelike Böhm opened the Café Adler in 1988, and for a year or so the oldest building in Kreuzberg sat overlooking Checkpoint Charlie and the Berlin Wall. The building's history, however, dates back to the 17th century, when it was a pharmacy called the Adler ('eagle'). The interiors have not been changed, and one of the rooms, with its original floors, ceiling and wallpaper, benefits from being maintained as a non-smoking space (smokers are asked to use the front room). In 2002 two of Böhm's employees – Nicola Brosch and Silke Meister – assumed ownership, but little else has changed. Adler is well known for its cakes, soups and hearty German cuisine, such as *geröstete Maultaschen*, an omelette filled with ravioli, which is in turn stuffed with meat and spinach.

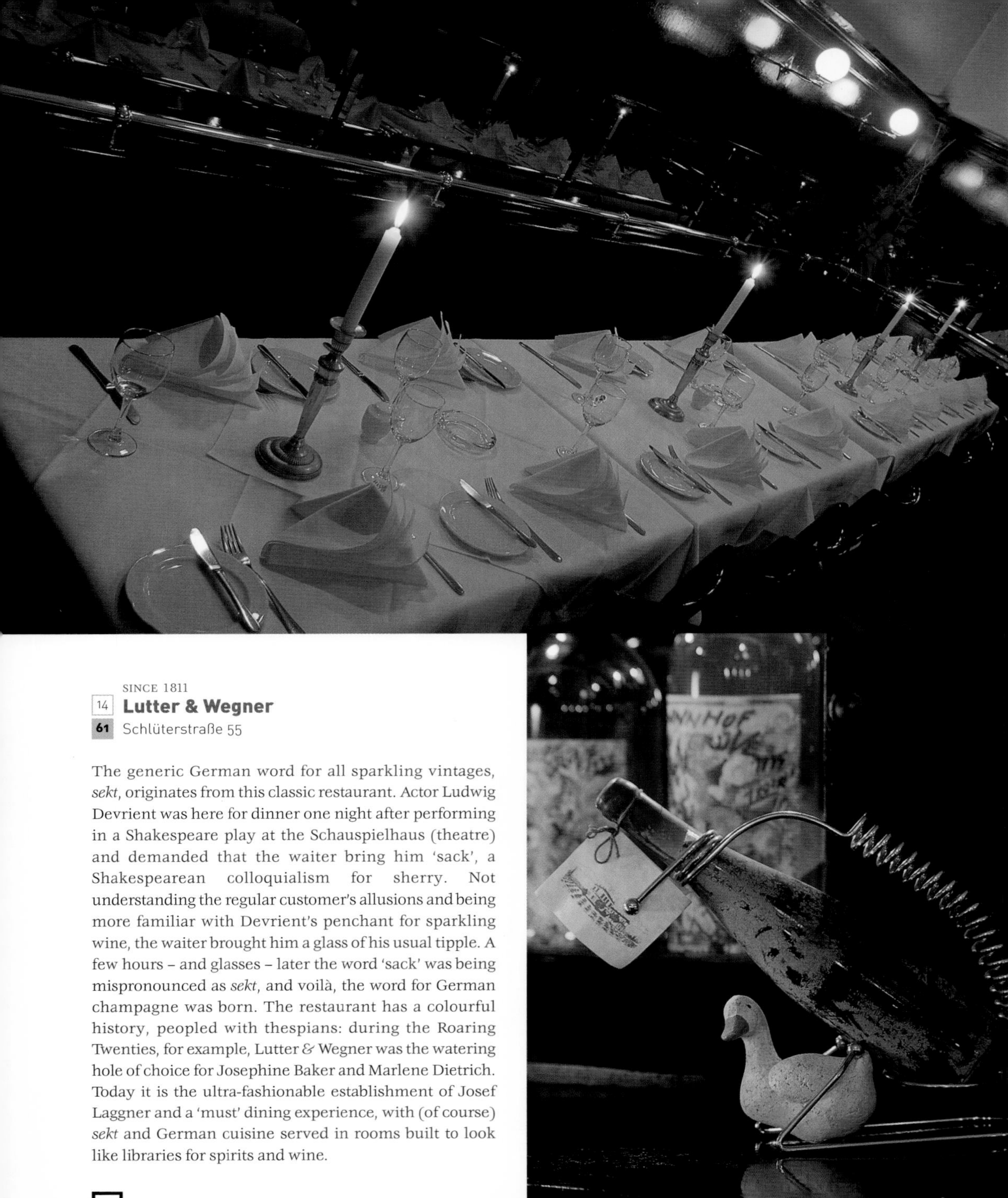

SINCE 1811

14 Lutter & Wegner

61 Schlüterstraße 55

The generic German word for all sparkling vintages, *sekt*, originates from this classic restaurant. Actor Ludwig Devrient was here for dinner one night after performing in a Shakespeare play at the Schauspielhaus (theatre) and demanded that the waiter bring him 'sack', a Shakespearean colloquialism for sherry. Not understanding the regular customer's allusions and being more familiar with Devrient's penchant for sparkling wine, the waiter brought him a glass of his usual tipple. A few hours – and glasses – later the word 'sack' was being mispronounced as *sekt*, and voilà, the word for German champagne was born. The restaurant has a colourful history, peopled with thespians: during the Roaring Twenties, for example, Lutter & Wegner was the watering hole of choice for Josephine Baker and Marlene Dietrich. Today it is the ultra-fashionable establishment of Josef Laggner and a 'must' dining experience, with (of course) *sekt* and German cuisine served in rooms built to look like libraries for spirits and wine.

OOH-LA-LA

88 Paris Bar

27 Kantstraße 152

Every capital city has a restaurant to which 'international superstars' (some real, some self-proclaimed) flock when they are in town. Since it opened in the 1960s, the Paris Bar has been just such a venue for Berlin. Because of its non-stop popularity, owner Michel Wurthle opened Le Bar du Paris Bar, a bistro-style sister eatery, next door, where it is possible to get a table without booking weeks in advance. Inside the Paris Bar German actor Otto Sander has an engraved plaque on the bar where he regularly sits. Art by regulars such as Martin Kippenberger, crowds every wall, and artists such as Christo, who once wrapped the entire Reichstag in fabric, animate the space itself. The menu is, not surprisingly, French bistro and includes terrific steaks, soups and accompaniments. Yet it is the action in the restaurant rather than on the plate that makes the Paris Bar the place it is. On a recent Friday night a young nude model walked through the restaurant to pose in the kitchen for local publication *Naked in Berlin*. Most diners ignored her.

COLOUR-CODED CLARET

Weinrot

Savoy Hotel, Fasanenstraße 9/10

The subject of a recent makeover by Kreativbüro Kessler + Kessler (see also Ku'Damm 101, p. 124), the Weinrot restaurant at the Savoy Hotel has been restored to its former glory. Fransziska and Daniel Kessler used oxblood red as the dominant colour scheme, in keeping with the hotel's house colour. Opulently decorated with crystal chandeliers, overstuffed red velvet chairs and gold banquettes, the room's décor contrasts with the huge glass façade (a listed Berlin monument subject to a protection order) and light polished parquet flooring to create an contemporary atmosphere, overlooked by the paintings of Berlin artist Horst Hirsig. The restaurant seats 60 and the neighbouring Salon Belvedere another 20. Frank Helms manages the food and beverages at the hotel, and keeps an evolving menu small, with traditional German dishes produced in light, appetizing portions. The wine list is – typically for Berlin – large, with a selection of 140 bottles

SPOT THE ARTISTE

14 Maxwell

9 Bergstraße 22

A genuine rags-to-riches story, Maxwell began as a restaurant in Kreuzberg, but protests from local riff-raff who thought it too sedate an 'establishment' drove it to Wilmersdorf. This displeased another set of locals who felt that it was too noisy and ensured that its lease was not renewed. Maxwell finally seems to have settled in a building remodelled by architect-regulars in the former Josty beer brewery in Mitte. The moves and uncertainty have paid off over time, and Maxwell today is a reservation-only, sophisticated eatery serving chef Uwe Popall's superlative fusion cuisine to Berlin's hip, wealthy, bright young things. The restaurant is set at the back of an awe-inspiring neo-Gothic building, and the courtyard is laid out to grass, with seating for 80 in the summer. Contemporary art pieces overlook two floors: Damien Hirst's minimal but colourful *Spots* is a perfect accompaniment to the cuisine and clientele.

HOMAGE TO AUSTRIA

88 **Ottenthal**

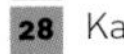

28 Kantstraße 153

Proprietor Arthur Schneller's hope was to create a tiny part of Austria in the heart of Berlin, and with his altar to Mozart and parts of an old church clock that once chimed in his native town of Ottenthal, he has succeeded in this delightful Austrian eaterie. Ottenthal is known for its vineyards, and Schneller's restaurant doubles as a wine shop selling regional vintages, with an astounding 250 wines from Austria's 16 wine regions. Typical dishes are Debreziner goulash with dumplings roasted in butter or a ragoût of genuine Austrian chamois with Brussels sprouts, bread dumplings and cranberries. And of course there is always the veal escalope, more commonly known as Wiener Schnitzel.

MORE THAN A BIRD

76 **Storch**

6 Wartburgstraße 54

Volker Hauptvogel's career is as colourful as his Alsatian restaurant. A typesetter by trade, he owned the infamous Pinguin Club until 1988. Having grown tired of the loud music and peanuts and cocktail sausages, he filled his time with music, typesetting and writing, but he missed the bustle of catering. When the lease of a corner sauna went unrenewed because of excessive on-site flesh-trading, Hauptvogel leapt at the chance to open his first proper restaurant. Decorated with enamel signs from old beer brands, it has a homey feel, which is further enhanced by the *Bier vom Fass* (beer on tap) and friend Andre Dock's house wine. The central dish is tarte flambé, an Alsatian brand of pizza that uses crème fraîche instead of tomato sauce for the topping. Hauptvogel's own favourites come with garnished with garlic, rocket or a typically Berlin preparation called *Eisbein*, which means 'pig leg'.

OLD PERFECTIONIST

88 Alt-Luxemburg

43 Windscheidtstraße 31

Karl Wannemacher opened his restaurant in honour of the tiny Benelux nation in 1982. Working hard to perfect his standard of cooking and imagination, he was rewarded for his efforts in 1988 with a Michelin star, which he retained for over a decade. In 1997 he was elected *Meisterkoch* (master chef), one of only eight in Berlin. With a predominantly German wine list he prepares French and, to a lesser degree, Benelux cuisine with his own innovative interpretations. Smoked eel terrine with horseradish, tomato millefeuilles with turbot, lobster and curry and monkfish in a saffron sauce are just a few of the variations on traditional dishes infused with a dash of Asian flavour – modern interpretations in a classic setting.

76 **Hugos**

2 Hotel Intercontinental, Budapester Straße 2

What was for many years the Zum Hugenotten restaurant on the ground floor of Berlin's five-star Intercontinental Hotel recently received a successful face-lift. In May 2003 it moved fourteen floors skyward and was remodelled by architect Alex Schulschenk as Hugos. Chef Thomas Kammeier, who trained as a baker and still refers to Wolfgang Dubs of Worms's Rotisserie Dubs as his mentor, began running the kitchen in 1998, receiving a Michelin star for his culinary craftsmanship. His dishes, which include a good number of fish choices, are light and fresh with a Mediterranean twist. Exiting the elevators, diners are greeted by wine-stocked cooling cabinets before entering the earth-toned restaurant. If you can take your eyes off the food, you will be rewarded with panoramic views across the Brandenburg Gate to Potsdamer Platz.

14

Dachgarten

67 Reichstag

The reimagined Reichstag (parliament building) is a proud and shining symbol of German unity. When it was first built by Paul Wallot in the 1890s, he could not have foreseen the 100 years of turbulent history that followed, culminating in the destruction of its fine cupola after the Second World War. A century later, British high-tech architect Norman Foster was asked to restore the building and cupola for the reunified government. His revolutionary design took the form of an all-glass cupola that swirls with visitors ascending its height to enjoy city-wide views and to peer down into the politicians' central debating chamber.

Though the cupola has become one of Berlin's main tourist attractions, fewer people know about the roof-top Dachgarden Restaurant, which has the double draw of gourmet cuisine and obligatory reservations that allow diners to jump the queue waiting to get to the roof. Lunch is the best time, as the cuisine is not as inspired as the architecture, and the breathtaking views come at a price.

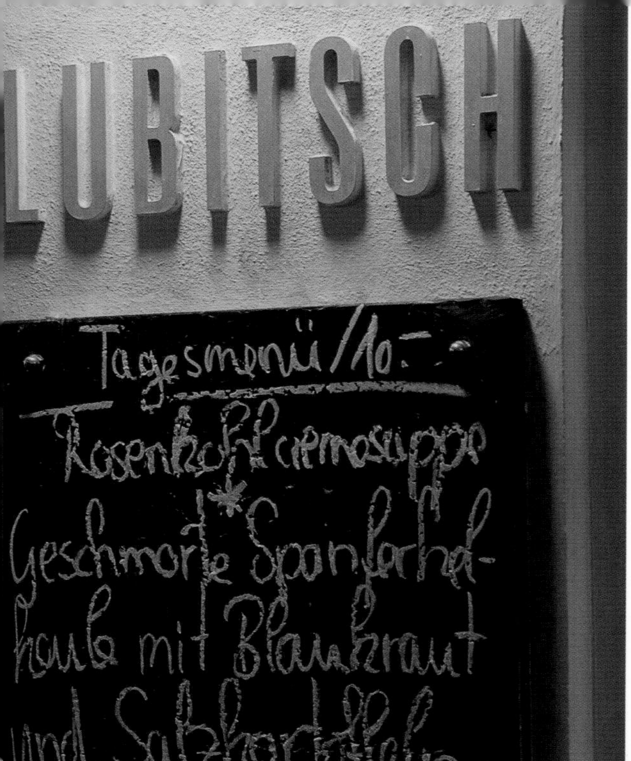

SOUL FOOD SECRET

Florian

29 Grolmanstraße 52

Ute Gielow and Gerti Hoffmann are the two friends who front what is now one of the most popular Berlin 'secrets' of specialist German soul food. When they opened in 1981 Florian was unique as a restaurant with a minimalist interior, drawing attention to the table rather than the décor surrounding it. Celebrities and artists make up the colourful clientele, who are known for donating their work to a slowly evolving art collection on the walls. The restaurant derives its noisy energy from the buzz of diners no doubt discussing gossip and politics, but the menu always provides a momentary conversation-stopper. Gielow and Hoffmann hail from Franken, the northern part of Bavaria, where 'Florian' fought for freedom in the 14th century, and the particularly refined German cuisine of that region is reflected in the menu. Hearty traditional dishes such as *Schweinebraten* (roast pork) and *Tafelspitz* (savoury boiled beef) and braised Nurnberg sausages are typical of the constantly changing offerings.

STAR IN THE ASCENDANT

Lubitsch

16 Bleibtreustraße 47

A Berlin institution owned by chef Florian Maria Schymczyk and art dealer Volker Diehl, Lubitsch was established in 1994. Schymczyk was already known to the upper echelons of German society, as he worked in the kitchen at the Berlin Golf and Country Club during the height of its pre-Wall popularity. Now he cooks his German dishes with 'an international touch' (think calves' liver with roasted onion and apple slices and creamed potato purée) privately and in this, his first restaurant, named after the German film director who used to live on the street but moved to Hollywood in 1943. One appreciative regular is Chancellor Schröder, who hires Schymczyk as chef for dinner parties of fifteen to twenty people at his home. Other famous fans include Prince Charles (Schymczyk cooked for him once when he was in Berlin) and late photographer Helmut Newton. Diehl also has a gallery in Mitte; his pieces adorn the walls of Lubitsch.

BREAD AND ROSES

58 Brot und Rosen

30 Am Friedrichshain 6

Peter Klanns's reputation for serving Italian food has spread by word of mouth. Even Chancellor Gerhard Schröder has been for dinner, as has British Prime Minister Tony Blair. In a city (like most) awash with Italian restaurants, Klanns's unique selling point is that he does it all himself, sourcing the freshest produce from suppliers he trusts and making his own organic oils. The interior is unfussy stark white with touches of Prussian grandeur in the form of cornicing and ornaments, all of which contrast with modern Déco photographic prints that Klanns selected. The restaurant benefits from a view over the pleasant Friedrichshain Park, which offers sylvan post-prandial refuge from the fashionable set spilling out of Brot und Rosen on to its terrace in warmer months.

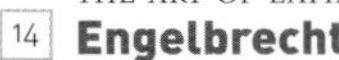

THE ART OF EATING

14 Engelbrecht

55 Schiffbauerdamm 6/7

Food artistry and a love of art are the common passions of husband and wife Florian and Jennifer Schüssler, as expressed in their restaurant Engelbrecht. He was training as a chef in Hannover's famous Clichy restaurant when he met Jennifer, whose background was also in hospitality. Via London and Paris they settled in Berlin in 1997, attracted by the idea of making their fresh start in a city that shared their attitude. Architect Accan Tesdorpf, who also worked on Ku'damm 101 (p. 124), retained the dark wood floor from the site's previous incarnation as the Zum Trichter restaurant (known for displaying Expressionist frescoes). The space divides into two rooms: the Grützke room, dominated by a huge Johannes Grützke portrait featuring Florian, his grandfather Emil, Jennifer and Johannes himself; and the Schröter room, named after Leipzig painter Anette Schröter, which overlooks the River Spree. The changing menu features typically German rollmop of red mullet with braised fennel as well as the simpler goat's-cheese gratin on chicory.

BRIGHT YOUNG THING

14 **Facil**

74 Potsdamer Straße 3

Michael Kempf is the youngest chef in Germany to be awarded a Michelin star (he was a mere 26 years old at the time) in recognition of the mastery he has gained in the kitchens of numerous starred restaurants. He is a culinary architect in a setting worthy of his skills. Located on the fifth floor of the Lauber & Wöhr–designed building, Facil is the in-house restaurant of the Madison Hotel (p. 116), although it stands alone as a glass house surrounded by an evergreen terrace. On honey-hued stone floors, the room is filled with semi-polished mahogany and light-shaded Donghia-upholstered chairs. Kempf offers a four-course menu with cheese or dessert or, for the gourmet, seven courses, alongside the changing à-la-carte menu. Foie gras with truffles, pine nut and apple coriander confit is one speciality; marinated scallops with melon and mint make a lighter starter. Main courses, such as 'variation of veal in two courses' or 'two variations of venison with cherries and celery', will delight even the most demanding palates.

SALT AND TOBACCO

58 Sale e Tabacchi

5 Kochstraße 18

Recognizable from the fronts of corner shops throughout Italy, the name of Piero de Vitis's second Berlin restaurant is an ironic reference to the habits of reporters (the staff of the daily newspaper *Tageszeitung* inhabit the building's upper floors). The restaurant's reputation is based on simple, fresh Italian cuisine, a theme that runs to Osteria No. 1 and Malatesta (p. 36), de Vitis's other eateries. Architect Max Dudler designed the interior, which is stylish and relaxed, thanks to the 6-metre- (20-foot-) high ceilings and covered terrace with lemon trees. The café has been an inspiration, and De Vitis knows his art and artists: Wilmer Koenig created a photomontage showing the restaurant when it is empty, which gives a clever impression of the room, and British artist Rachel Whiteread is a friend. He cares very much about every detail, for example sourcing a coffee called Andreatrinci from a small coffee-manufacturing family who for ten years were the private coffee providers for Benetton.

drink

Drinking is truly a 24-hour activity in Berlin. Continental café culture is fuelled by coffee drunk throughout the day, and, as one of the few cities in Europe that has no state-imposed time after which drinks may not be served, the capital is well served by watering holes of all varieties, beer gardens (in summer), high-concept futuristic lounge bars, bohemian hideaways and grunge-trendy early-morning spots. It is not surprising to see a well-dressed lady on her own ordering a glass of champagne at 11 a.m. or to wind up the night drinking shots with an intellectual-chat chaser at 7 a.m., all a piece of Berlin's history and celebratory attitude towards booze since the Roaring Twenties.

UNDERWATER LOVE

 58 **Cream**

 25 Schlesische Straße 6

Watergate

Falckensteinstraße 49

A smooth neutral space, large and light, overlooking the Spree with ultramodern clean-living décor might mislead visitors into believing that Cream is an exclusive nightspot, but it is in fact a great riverside place for good coffee. Cream roasts its own beans, and the atmosphere is relaxed, welcoming and warm. Sunlight floods the dining space through a huge glass river-view façade. Close by is Watergate, a nightclub whose key nod to design is that it is partially situated at water level, allowing for clean vistas across the Spree's surface. Watergate's music is at the cutting edge of the techno and drum 'n' base circuit, attracting DJs from all over Germany and the world to spin for frenzied dancers.

MORE THAN A NICE CUP OF TEA

14 Tadschikische Teestube/Die Möwe

66 Palais am Festungsgraben, Am Festungsgraben 1

Built in 1753 as the Palais Donna to house Friedrich the Great's principal servant, the huge Palais am Festungsgraben on Unter den Linden later became the seat of the Prussian ministers of finance and remained in their control until 1853. During the 1920s it was a popular Berlin salon and the meeting place of intellectuals and their acolytes, and as one of the few buildings practically untouched by Allied bombing, it enjoyed a postwar role as the house of German–Soviet friendship. Today it houses three ballrooms (red, blue and yellow) and, illuminated by a chandelier the size of a VW Beetle, all are available for hire. There is an artists' dining club called Die Möwe (The Seagull) and what is probably the palace's highlight for visitors: the wonderfully bizarre Tadschikische Teestube (Tajik Tearoom), with an entire interior from Tajikistan (a present from the former Soviet state to the DDR), in which shoes must be removed before sitting down on enormous cushions to take tea served from samovars.

PARK LIFE

76 Café am Neuen See

20 Lichtensteinallee 2

In the heart of the Tiergarten, overlooking the Neuen See on one side and the Zoologischer Garten on the other, is Berlin's largest beer garden. Arriving on foot, by bicycle or on one of the boats that can be hired on the lake, guests take up one of Café am Neuen See's 1,500 seats to enjoy the largely unlandscaped natural surroundings. The park feels rather wild and woody in places – in a Caspar David Friedrich kind of way – which is perhaps why it is somewhat deserted in the winter. The park was once the hunting ground of Prussian royalty, who released animals into it and chased them for sport (hence Tiergarten, 'animal garden'). The wild animals are still there, of course, now all safely tucked up in the zoo.

BEER BARREL

76 Felsenkeller

7 Akazienstraße 2

In 1993 Günter During and Michaela Friedrichs took over an establishment that had been in existence since 1920 and whose period shipping paraphernalia still stand as reminders. 'We changed some of the pictures when we came here, but the clients remained the same,' remarks Friedrichs. There have been only five owners since it opened, which is why a major renovation has never taken place, and it is that continuity that ensures Felsenkeller's charm. An old cigarette display cabinet houses original packets (not for sale) of Player's Navy Cut cigarettes. Enamelled posters on the walls bear time-specific slogans, such as 'Hamburg-Amerika Line', 'Cunard Line Vertretung Hier USA & Canada' and 'Smoke Player's Navy Cut Cigarettes'. The bar tenders have beer-tapping down to a fine art here: pils will proudly wear what Germans believe to be the perfect head, which if executed correctly, takes seven minutes to pour and ends up looking like a frothy cappuccino.

IN A CITY GARDEN

44 Pratergarten
5 Hecht Club

Kastanienallee 7–9

Berlin's oldest beer garden is famous for the way it celebrates the German love of beer, talk and outdoor drinking. Set off behind the busy Kastanienallee, the venue is shielded from the main road by trees, evoking the genuine sense of being in a garden. Packed in the warmer months, it was regularly closed down by the police in pre-1989 days, but it reopened in 1996, and now even in the winter its two barn-like *Bierhalle* are stuffed with beer-swilling locals. In summer lucky guests are entertained by musicians and occasional street cabaret artists, acts that have attracted actor Willem Dafoe and designer Vivienne Westwood, to name a few. But there's more: located behind an old open-air stage in the garden is Hecht Club, a semi-secret little cocktail bar and place for clandestine encounters. Inside, the décor is the fantastical re-creation of a film set 'a là James Bond', whose 1960s feel attains its zenith in the design of the bar, with its white curved ceilings and plush furnishings and lights. Do phone ahead, as its small size means Hecht Club is often rented for private parties.

WHAT'S BEHIND?

76 Green Door

13 Winterfeldtstraße 50

The slogan announcing 'The Power of Positive Drinking', sets the tone for a long night of cocktail drinking behind the Green Door of Fritz Müller-Scherz's exclusive drinking den. It is exclusive only because you have to buzz on the wrong side of a large, green padded door and undergo an inspection through a keyhole before you are admitted (or not). Should you make the grade, you will be ushered into a small space whose curving walls and bare wood-grain wall heighten a feeling of uncertain curiosity that this establishment exudes. The interior is the work of three architect pals of Müller-Scherz, who is familiar in Berlin as the screenwriter of the Wim Wenders film *Der Amerikanische Freund (The American Friend)*, starring Dennis Hopper, and *World on a Wire*. He opened Green Door on the site of Berlin's legendary Havanna Bar and has retained the cigar-selling tradition and humidor.

JE T'AIME

88 Gainsbourg

30 Savignyplatz 5

This bar's loyal neighbourhood following often makes it impossible to find space at the bar, let alone an empty table, even on Monday nights at 1 a.m. Though some newcomers to the city might ask, 'Doesn't Berlin ever work?', here one man's poison is another man's profit. Owner Friedhelm 'Frido' Keiling celebrated ten years of pint-pulling in 2003, and has a band that always plays at the Fête de la Musique, a free city-wide musical jam held in participating bars, clubs, restaurants and even public gardens, which starts annually on Midsummer's Eve. Keiling conceived the bar's design and named it after his hero, the great French singer Serge Gainsbourg, who died the year of the bar's opening.

BOXING RING

88 **Diener Tattersall**

31 Grolmanstraße 47

Located by the local stables, this dining room was once used by local gentry for sustenance when they returned from equestrian jaunts. In the 1950s it was acquired by a famous boxer, and since then has become the hang-out for young sportsmen, film celebrities and the ladies who have a taste for them. Today its walls are covered in faces from the past, mostly black-and-white photos dedicated to the restaurant, with expressions of enjoyment and best wishes. The place has a smoky allure and, though the average age of visitors is over 50, all share in the worldly ambience. Actors Ulrich Tukur, Mario Adorf and Detlef Buck all peer down on the eating and drinking below, for Diener Tattersall has a kitchen as well, serving genuine German cuisine. It is not for the faint-hearted: the *Königsberger Klöpse*, presented on an oval plate, consists of three huge meatballs sitting on a mound of potatoes (beet salad on the side), which might just be the best fare with which to line your stomach before a long night ahead.

DR ZHIVAGO

44 Pasternak

18 Knaackstraße 22–24

Boris Pasternak, author of *Dr Zhivago*, won the Nobel Prize for Literature in 1958. Before the Second World War Berlin was home to a large Russian Jewish community, with Pasternak living among them, between 1905 and 1906 and again later, in the 1920s. This restaurant was named in his honour by another Russian Jew, Ilja Kaplan, who moved to Berlin in 1990 to seek his fortune. Some

the quartet. Situated next door to a synagogue, the restaurant was a passport office during DDR times, before Kaplan remodelled it to resemble the writer's living room in the 1930s, an entirely fitting backdrop to traditional *borscht* and *pelmini*. He is most proud of his mossberry vodka, made from a Siberian fruit berry and infused into pure potato vodka.

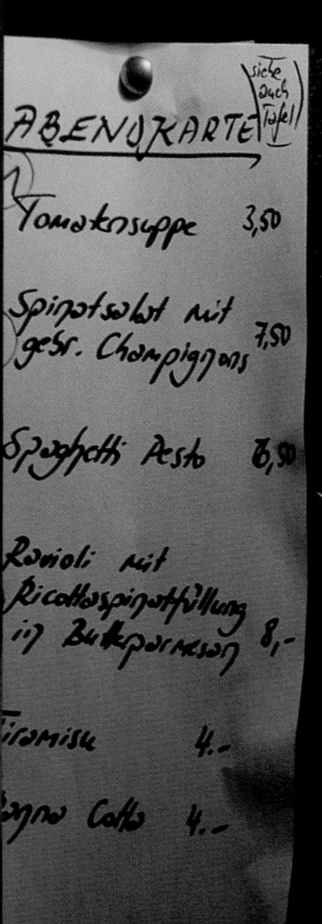

CHEESE TREES

58 Würgeengel

22 Dresdener Straße 122

The tastefully decorated Würgeengel bar took its name from Luis Buñuel's cult film *El Angel Exterminador* and is one of Kreuzberg's nightlife highlights. Crowded, smoky, noisy and alive on any given evening, the interior combines red velvet furniture with a beautiful stucco ceiling whose depth is doubled by the gilt-edged mirrors that adorn the walls. Students, artists, cinema-goers and barflies mix in this combustible atmosphere. Many choose to combine a drink here with a visit to the adjacent Gorgonzola Club restaurant, which serves Italian food in the stark interior of an early 1900s building. Both venues are accessible through their own street entrances, but are also connected by a tiny 'secret' passage – useful when the bar spills over.

ALL FOR ONE AND ONE FOR ALL

76

Kumpelnest 3000

15 Lützowstraße 23

This bar is the great equalizer. Dames and dukes, guys and dolls, ladies and gentlemen, tramps and pimps – all are present and accounted for in the lively mix that frequents Kumpelnest 3000 from about 1 a.m. onward on any given early morning of the week (anyone arriving earlier will find the place empty). Kumpelnest is the last alcoholic port of call at the end of a long night of revelry, so expect to meet anyone and everyone if you go there when activity reaches its peak at sunrise. The crazy broken-glass mosaic on the walls, dusty overstuffed sofas and the stools that line the bar mirror the incongruous assortment that is the clientele. This place is not for the sober – never expect to remember – or be remembered by – all your new 'best friends'.

BE STILL, MY BEATING HEART

58 **Rote Harfe/Orient Lounge**

15 Oranienstraße 3

Once the happening place for heavy-metal moshers and biker boys, this venue underwent a sophisticated face-lift and reinvented itself as the playground of pretty little girls and their handsome escorts. The first floor has been dedicated to Moorish-inspired lounge life under the banner of 'Orient Lounge'. Rouge – on the walls and the faces – adds to the sultry air of Middle Eastern intrigue that is spun from low-level cushioned sofas and soft dappled opaque light effects. Unusually for Berlin, the staff sometimes exercises a door policy, probably more an indication of the club's full-to-bursting capacity than for 'face control.'

SOMETHING SPECIAL

88 **Galerie Bremer**

6 Fasanenstraße 37

Originally from Surinam, Rudolf van der Lak moved to Berlin over fifty years ago and married Anja Bremer. 'My wife was a very strong woman and we knew a lot of artists. She wanted to find a space where we would all be comfortable.' Enter Galerie Bremer, which has hosted some of the world's most established artists and their collectors since its inception in 1946. Picasso ceramics and the work of other big names have passed through the space. But the gallery is also unusual because its meeting point is a circular bar in the back room, most often manned by van der Lak himself (despite the fact that he is getting on a bit, having been born in 1920). He is a delightful gentleman who loves to talk about the work that he and Bremer have done together over the years. Sadly she died in 1986 but van der Lak is keeping her art, culture and social legacy alive. 'We've been here for over fifty years and I am planning on staying another fifty.'

NUMERICAL VALUES

58 **Q3A**

32 Stralauer Allee 2c

Club 12/34

Stralauer Allee 1

Occupying a former egg-storage warehouse, Q3A serves up unadorned modern cuisine in unembellished surroundings. Large glass windows afford diners views over the Spree, and in the summer a large terrace and its deck chairs are occupied by locals watching the sun melt into the urban horizon. After sundown, those who have not sunk into a lazy stupor might tumble over to Club 12/34, a nightclub offering a blend of national and international DJs spinning mellow techno alongside fashion and music events in support of Berlin's local creative scene.

BARFLY

58

CSA Bar

28 Karl-Marx-Allee 96

This site on the grand Karl-Marx-Allee was once East Berlin's branch office for the flight bookings of CSA, the Czech Republic's national airline. Although the name remains the same, the escapism on offer is rather different these days. One of the first and perhaps best of the social venues to take advantage of the breathtaking Communist gigantism of the grand boulevard, CSA Bar is a night-time venue that features a stunning interior, stark linear bar and colour provided by the galaxy of liquor bottles that line its back wall. White tones set a relaxed and very hip atmosphere, a stark contrast to the architectural dereliction in this part of the city. Unquestionably a destination.

THEATRE OF THE PEOPLE

22 6 Volksbühne: Roter Salon and Grüner Salon

Rosa-Luxemburg-Platz 2

Frank Castorf is resident director at the 'People's Theatre', renowned for its nonconformist performances. Housed in an impressive columned building set back from its neighbours, it stands alone, an imposing monolith. It was established by master theatre-builder Oskar Kaufmann in 1913 as the second of six theatres he was to design in Berlin before he fled to Palestine in 1933 (his first was the Hebbel-Theater, p. 65). Destroyed during the Second World War and reopened in 1954, the Volksbühne is today home to two contemporary salons, the Roter (Red) Salon and the Grüner (Green) Salon. The Roter Salon's presents hip drum 'n' base for frenzied dancers and spectators; the Grüner Salon, on the other side of the building, is a more

MY NAME IS HELMUT

Newton Bar

62 Charlottenstraße 57

Both the location overlooking the Gendarmenmarkt and the cool interior scream success for this decadently opulent cocktail bar, which was opened by Lutter & Wegner (see also p. 130) in 1999. Inside are huge prints by eponymous photographer Helmut Newton, featuring practically life-size images of his (signature) naked women, wearing only high-heeled shoes, which lends the entire bar a slight air 1980s nostalgia – which is no bad thing. The decade of excess acts as a stimulant for the Newton Bar's clientele, most of whom look as if they enjoyed a few excesses back then. The décor too is sophisticated, with big mirrors, dark lacquered walls and marble flooring. On the first floor there is a cigar club and smoking room that can be booked for private functions. The cocktail list is impressive, as it should be. Martinis and the whisky selection are recommended.

CUE THE MUSIC

Qiu

73 Potsdamer Straße 3

Lutz Hesse took his idea for a lounge bar to Hamburg-based Flum Design with a brief to impart an oriental ambience to a somewhat spartan modern building that is part of the DaimlerChrysler quarter overlooking the Potsdamer Platz. Situated on the first floor of the Madison Hotel (p. 116), Qiu is not obvious from street level. Overlooking the neon-lit Sony Centre, with dangling fabric chandeliers, a permanent waterfall running ceiling to floor over golden mosaic tiles and ornamental dark-red roses, cocktails are accompanied by a sophisticated selection of appetizers: imperial pigeon with balsamic lentils; seaweed risotto with grey mullet; duck croquettes; and gazpacho with strawberries and scallops.

EIN MANUFAKTUR-PRODUKT DER BLINDENANSTALT VON BERLIN . ORANIENSTRASSE 26 . 10997 BERLIN . TEL. 030 25886614 . Fax 030 25886615
DIE IMAGINÄRE MANUFAKTUR.
HOUSEBRUSH
DESIGN:
ALEXANDRA MARTINI
HENRIKE MEYER

shop

The city's attitude toward shopping is all about the individual, if not the idiosyncratic. Little boutiques sprinkle neighbourhoods, often run by only one or two people and consisting of a retail outlet fronting studio workspaces at the back. Wandering into these shops usually means meeting the maker of most of what lies within. With their fingers on the pulse of Berlin culture, designers are not committed to producing collections by the season and can react to demands as they arise, a useful skill in Berlin's dynamic shoppingscape. Owners take personal satisfaction in discussing their work, so visitors to the shops below might emerge versed in the history of the cocoa bean or having heard the milliner's tale first-hand.

ALL DAY I DREAM ABOUT SPORT

14 **adidas Originals Store**

45 Münzstraße 13–15

This mega international sneaker success story began with one man, Adi (Adolf) Dassler, who was born in Germany in 1900 and over the 77 years of his life built a tiny shoe factory into a global sporting-goods brand. He made his first pair of shoes in his mother's washroom in 1920 and opened the first factory with brother Rudolf in 1924. He shod the feet of the German national team at the 1936 Berlin Olympics. When the brothers fell out in 1948, Rudolf formed the rival Puma sportswear label and Adi founded Adidas and registered his 'three stripes' as the now familiar trademarked logo in 1949. During the 1960s and 1970s the label diversified to encompass accessories, tracksuits and sporting equipment. After Dassler's death, his son Horst continued the family tradition until he, too, died in 1987. By 1990 Adidas was no longer a family-run enterprise, but the legend lives on through the personalities it sponsors and, most recently, its new concept stores. The Berlin branch is one of only two in Germany.

TRIPPING THE LIGHT FANTASTIC

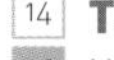

14 Trippen

34 Hackesche Höfe, Rosenthaler Straße 40/41

Michael Oehler and Angela Spieth were frustrated (he financially, she creatively) shoe designers who met in Berlin in 1990 and pooled forces to create an original approach to footwear. The name Trippen, an Old Germanic word for the wooden protective slip-on shoes worn over less durable silky varieties during the Middle Ages, suited the duo perfectly as the company has become internationally synonymous with wooden-soled footwear since its foundation in 1994. Initially, it was financial necessity that forced them to make wooden shoes, and they struggled until comfortable, durable and eco-friendly footwear began to stride into the mainstream. When demand for the Trippen shoe took off, they patented their sole and natural shape; even today, Oehler and Spieth depend on a network of small, family-run shoe-making companies to manufacture their product. The niche brand is reflected in their stores, whose décor is plain and functional to keep the focus firmly on the footwear.

MILLINER EXTRAORDINAIRE

14 Fiona Bennett

51 Große Hamburger Straße 25

She could hardly have a more English name, but Miss Bennett is definitely a Berliner. Born to a British father and a German mother, she has lived in the city since she was six. Her three-year millinery training at Dama Hutton was traditional but stood her in good stead as a contender for the crown of Berlin hat designers. A love of performance art meant her early collections were often in novel formats that gained her attention and a loyal clientele. With friend Elisabeth Prantner (of Lisa D., see p. 29), she did between 30 and 40 shows a year: they once hired a ghost train and the audience rode carts past performers wearing Bennett's hats and Prantner's clothes. Now her creative imagination is expressed in her shop, a lilac and mint-green space that exists solely to display her head sculptures and hats on 'stages'. There are trilbies and bowlers for men, felt caps for daywear and coral and flower replicas constructed from feathers. Her elegant 'sting-ray' hat is crafted from almost 4,000 tiny feathers that appear to move when they catch the light.

ROSES ARE RED

14 **Cara Tonga**

41 Dircksenstraße 51

Lars Scherbarth and Jens Büchner are to floristry what sculpture is to the art world. Under a name as original as their creations they make flower art and deliver it daily to Gucci, Hermès, KaDeWe, Prada and the exclusive private clubs of Berlin. Neither comes from a conventional floristry background, as is apparent from their imaginative, architectural flower arrangements and their use of unusual components, such as Australian dead wood, which opens up and explodes its seeds when burnt, or dried-out coconut palms placed at an angle under light so that the shadow forms part of the effect. Scherbarth and Büchner occasionally use more popular flowers, but even their roses look as if they have been dipped in polychromatic paint pots. To visit either of their two premises in Berlin is to take a language lesson in horticulture – Heliconia, lotus, banana, ginger, orchid, calla and artichoke in all their combinations delight the mind as well as the senses.

IN AND OUT

14 **Breathe**

17 Rochstraße 17

After a decade working for the Lancaster Group, Gregor Vidzer was ready to open his own cosmetic-care boutique. With a design by RoomSafari (p. 49), he and Sven Eric Moos created a beauty haven that delights first eye, then nose and finally the soul. 'All the products have a story, because I stock only niche, natural brands,' explains Vidzer. The owners encourage customers to experiment with pigment palettes, creams or perfume bottles, and the high-ceilinged space enhances the experience: mirrors can be pulled away from the walls, make-up stands are positioned in the centre of the shop. Dark sea-grass matting covers the floor, but Breathe's white walls are light and the space smells freshly masculine. Although there is make-up by Bloom and skincare by Julisis, it is obvious that the boys' real passion is perfume – they sell a custom-made variety by Swedish parfumier Sissel Tolaas, who concocts an individual scent for each of its patrons.

ÜBER FASHION ICON

14 **Claudia Skoda**

24 Alte Schönhauser Straße 35

Claudia Skoda has been around: her move from Ku'damm to Mitte in 2002 was the most visible signal that this sector of Berlin was *the* place to be for fashion shops, style setters, designers, artists and photographers. But Skoda is now in her sixties, and her story started in 1970s Kreuzberg. For years her legendary knitwear took her to New York, where she had a store on Soho's Thompson Street and clothed David Bowie and Tina Turner. Immediately identifiable, Skoda is known for comfortable knitwear for men and women that fits the human form. Certain weaves mimic muscles and shape the contours of the wearer's body. Skoda draws attention to these lines and curves without having to reveal skin, and as such her work is enigmatically erotic. Her classic lines use multicoloured stretch knitwear, but her recent repertoire embraces angora, viscose, linen, acetate, alpaca, kid mohair and elastane. One piece is a flowing, metallically shimmering dress that hangs so heavily that the wearer must walk with careful elegance.

NADA NOUGHT

14 NIX

29 Heckmannhöfe, Oranienburger Straße 32

A play on the German word *nichts* (nothing), Barbara Gebhardt's label is designed with subtle anonymity. Her clothes do not scream any particular style but are smart, wearable, durable and functional. This simple ethic has established her as one of Berlin's most respected fashion designers. Using mostly natural tones (there is an occasional nod to printed fabrics: Nordic reindeer for a winter collection, for example) and stretchy, comfortable cotton-Lycra textiles, Gebhardt makes suits, skirts, trousers and jackets for men, women and children. The detail is playful, but look deeper and you will find evidence of her true tailoring skills: a tuck here and a cut there that can make the piece. Her practical imagination is most evident in her accessory range: fleece-wool hats with ear flaps so long they grow into scarves and fingerless gloves that rise above the elbow, becoming sleeves in their own right.

14 HOT HATS

Hut Up

28 Oranienburger Straße 32

Famous for its vivacious pinks and effervescent oranges, Hut Up's colour range spans over 125 shades that are used in Christine Birkle's felt creations. Although *Hut* means 'hat', Birkle has not limited her design talents to headwear – silk, organza and muslin are woven intricately together with pure merino wool into seamless garments. So popular is her original style that Birkle's work is now sold in Japan, England, France Italy and the United States. Nor does she limit herself to women's wear: in fact, it was her baby collection and accessories for nurseries that caught the attention of buyers from Donna Karan, Hermès and Dries van Noten; Karan sells Birkle's egg-warmers (brightly coloured felt affairs that could pass as elf's hats) in her New York 'Home' store. The Hut Up shop also features felt cushions, glass and hot-water-bottle holders, solid plush teddy bears and a delightful one-piece baby snuggle-crib available in powder-puff pink or sky blue.

Berlinomat

29 Frankfurter Allee 89

The economic climate for independent designers in Berlin in 2003 was rather grey: the city was in debt and with a zero-percent growth rate. It was thus with great optimism that Jörg Wichmann and Theresa Meirer opened their space selling fashion, jewelry, art, furniture and product design, all from locals – in September that year. They began by recruiting over sixty designers (the number keeps growing) and were stunned by how much talent they discovered. 'The notion of selling underrepresented work under one roof was immediately celebrated by everyone we approached,' Wichman says. Going from strength to strength, Berlinomat is now an outlet for the couple's own fashion and jeanswear label, Hotinaf. Wichmann and Meirer share the 280 square-metre (3,000 -square-foot) space with betonWare's concrete furniture, Dreigold's jewelry and Extratapete's wallpaper – to name only a few – and an organic café that adds up to a total shopping experience.

SMOKING AND DRINKING

14 Whisky & Cigars

50 Sophienstraße 23

Two women met regularly to play chess, smoke cigars and drink whisky. Experiencing poor availability in Mitte drew their attention to a gap in the market and within three months, Lisa von Treskow and Eva Sichelschmidt had set up shop, surrounded by the amber glow of back-lit bottles and the moist scent of unburned tobacco. Products are displayed on shelves categorized by country, creating an veritable library of whiskies. The large selection of aged single malts, including special bottlings, are numbered by the bottle and cask on their label, making them as rare as a limited-edition print. Treskow left to run a paper shop, RSVP Papier in Mitte (p. 172), but Sichelschmidt built the range to some 400 whiskies and a rich choice of Cuban, Dominican, Honduran, Nicaraguan and Jamaican tobacco rolls. There is a small bar for tasting, and she hosts whisky seminars. All of this happens in a cosy 1920s-style environment designed to create an ambience ideal for lighting up a fine cigars and sipping the amber nectar.

WINERY

44 Weinerei

26 Veteranenstraße 14

With family histories steeped in wines and spirits, Jürgen Stumpf and Philippe Gross have a cult following that was consolidated with Weinerei, the Prenzlauer Berg wine shop they opened in 1997. Gross's parents are wine producers based in northern Bavaria and their vineyard supplies bottles to the Weinerei cellar; Stumpf's cousin makes the fruit schnapps that are sold in elegantly hand-labelled bottles under the name of Mirabellen. To accompany their liquid assets, they opened an unconventional no-name café across the street that operates on a trust system in which home-made tarts and puddings are left all day long on a counter for customers to help themselves and leave payment in an open bowl. So far the system has worked, and rumour has it that the idea has been extended to a restaurant around the corner that serves duck and fish.

ORGIASTIC FOOD FEST

88 KaDeWe

24 Tauentzienstraße 21–24

When the shopper approaches the doors of KaDeWe, those who worship at the altar of consumerism can anticipate emotions akin to those of a devout Catholic on a first visit to the Vatican. International shopaholics may already know that this monolithic mecca, the Kaufhaus des Westens, or 'Department Store of the West', is the largest department store on mainland Europe. Built by the Jewish entrepreneur Adolf Jandorf in 1907, it comprises seven floors crammed with the latest labels and answer-to-ageing creams. Its crowning glory is the Food Hall on the sixth floor (the seventh is the Wintergarten restaurant). Visit it on Saturday afternoon to see locals and tourists competing at the national sport of eating. Every counter is accompanied by a food bar. Live fish swimming in tanks, innocently awaiting their culinary fate; a Bols cocktail bar; champagne bars, oyster and salad bars, a crêperie, Wurst houses, a pâtisserie and a chocolaterie: this is consumption at its most decadent and indulgent. Whatever your taste-buds desire, they cannot fail to be satiated at KaDeWe.

CHOCOLATE FACTORY

76 Chocolaterie Estrellas

8 Akazienstraße 21

After training at chocolate company Most, Esther Kurtz plucked up the courage to go it alone, setting up a little chocolate factory and giving it a Spanish-influenced name because 'all the cocoa plantations are in Spanish-speaking countries'. Kurtz uses traditional methods to manufacture chocolate figures and to develop her own recipes. She sources cocoa from a Venezuelan plantation that produces a mild flavour, allowing her to keep the cocoa concentration high, at about 70% minimum, and still be appealing to children. Cocoa blocks and almond paste come from Lübeck, which is famous for these delicacies and nougat. To these ingredients Kurtz adds spices, chilli and German molasses, which is rich in iron but contains no sugar (it was the lifeblood of Berlin after the Second World War). Although her space is small, Kurtz does all her work in its back room, stocking her shelves with her own figurines and Berlinoise, a paste made from hazelnuts, chocolate and cream, as well as items by her favourite chocolate makers, many of whom are now friends.

CHOCOLATE ADDICT

44 In't Veld Schokoladen

21 Dunckerstraße 10

Holger In't Veld loves chocolate so much that he opened his own space, a personal homage to the cocoa bean. Filled with the finest chocolate brands in the world, In't Veld Schokoladen and its owner offer an education on the cocoa varieties that is equivalent to the experience of drinking fine wine. In't Veld sources his stock mainly from family companies with a history of producing hand-made chocolate. The Bonnat family in the French Alps near Grenoble, for example, use the same machines their forefathers did in 1884 to process the beans from their own plantations on the Ivory Coast. The result is a slightly coarse mix of cocoa, sugar and cocoa butter. Mack Domori is an Italian choco-fiend, who lives on a Venezuelan plantation and inscribes on each of his wrappers, 'I wish to be a cocoa bean.' In't Veld also sells Berliner Erich Hamann's beautifully packaged chocolate. Hamann once had ten shops in pre-war Berlin: today his three bitter and one milk varieties are crafted from original recipes and are notoriously rich.

CHOCOLATE LOVE STORY

88 Melanie

36 Goethestraße 4

This delightful tale of delectable edibles begins in 1953 when Eberhard Päller was training as a pâtissier in his native Zwickau in Saxony, former east Germany. While voyaging on a merchant ship between 1957 and 1960 his eyes were opened to the delights of exotic ingredients. When a certain Madame Melanie offered him a shop space in 1968, he decided to create a venue for the faraway products he had seen and the recipes he had in mind for them. The result is a gourmet paradise that today houses over 4,000 articles, with imported treasures from as far away as Colombia and Vietnam, as well as a range of German specialities practically extinct in modern outlets, such as *Agnessen* cookies, *Seelchen* and *Spionle*. Pride of place is occupied by the 89 (and counting) types of truffle, all of them invented and made by Päller and 21 of which are unique. Curry, mace, coriander, absinthe and orange-mustard are some of the unlikely flavours he has blended into his own chocolate creations.

RETURN TO SENDER

14 RSVP Papier in Mitte

11 Mulackstraße 14

It was the practical, professional restrictions faced by Lisa von Treskow as a working graphic designer in her native Berlin that awakened her to the need for a shop selling fine paper and stationery accessories. She had found a similar lack before opening Whisky & Cigars (p. 168) with Eva Sichelschmidt, 'but I stopped drinking,' Treskow says. Thus RSVP took root on Mulackstraße in 2000. Fine papers, envelopes and writing tools are precisely laid out on a floor-to-ceiling wooden shelving unit, which must be examined from all sides and at all levels to see what Treskow has chosen. 'Moleskin books are currently *en vogue*, as van Gogh, Matisse and Bruce Chatwin once wrote in such notebooks.' (The covers may look like moleskin but are in fact made of plastic.) Here you can find Swiss Caran d'Ache pens that will cover 600 sheets of scribbling without leaking or running out. Treskow discovered that her heavy-silver scissors manufacturer in Italy supplies the same model to the Gucci brand. 'Mine cost 15 euros and theirs are 120,' she points out, 'which makes one Gucci logo worth 105 euros.' Meike Wander took over RSVP in 2004.

URBAN DIMENSION

14 Pro QM

21 Alte Schönhauser Straße 48

An open forum for discussion and debate, supported by an outstanding library of books on architecture, town planning, politics, design and art theory and practice, Pro QM is the brainchild of Jesko Fezer, Katja Reichard and Axel Wieder and has become one of the city's most important centres for architectural discussion. The three Berliners – all professional architects, theorists and artists – had worked together on city policy before finding the location for Pro QM in a former butcher's shop. Fezer took on the task of redesigning the space but left the beautiful Eastern European ceramic tiles on the walls. The focus of the texts is urbanism ('pro qm' means 'per square metre', a reference to the modern measure of urban space), specifically the idea that a city is not just a built-up area but a space of culture and ideas, meeting and development. The venue has become more of a hobby for the owners, who continue to hold genuine influence on Berlin's dynamic urban evolution through their private practice.

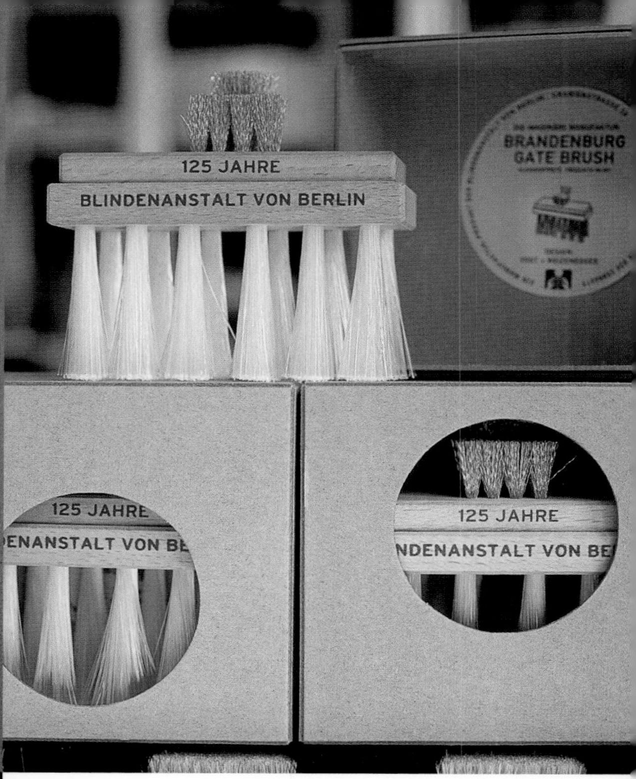

THE IMAGINARY FACTORY

58 Die Imaginäre Manufaktur (DIM)

20 Oranienstraße 26

Imagine: respected designers conceiving innovative products, all using brushes, and the materials for brushes hand-crafted by the Blindenanstalt von Berlin (Institute for the Blind), who have been making brushes on this site since 1876. Die Imaginäre Manufaktur (DIM, 'The Imaginary Factory') began as an experiment by designers Oliver Vogt and Hermann Weizenegger and was originally directed by Peter Bergmann. Their mission to create unconventional brooms and brushes with and for Berlin's blind has proved an astonishing success, celebrated at design shows and exhibitions as far afield as London, Milan, New York and Tokyo. Recent designs from Tim Parsons, Alex Kufus, MotorBerlin and Max Wolf, among others, have included prototypes whose manufacture has raised the profile and the self-esteem of the people who work there. Adhering to the ethos that new products should serve old functions, products are well made, clever and quirky – wicker coat-hangers, bread baskets incorporating a coffee cup – and timeless – like the original brushes and brooms.

retreat

Greater Berlin encompasses a vast metropolitan area dotted with pockets of natural landscape. Venture to the border of the official city limits, and visitors will find other worlds, some almost entirely untouched by the ravages of history that have given the city so much of its character. From the cultural treasure that is Potsdam to yesteryear's playgrounds of royal young bloods, from a dip in the Baltic to a trip down politically loaded memory lane, there are excursions from the city to cater to all tastes and sensibilities.

SUBURBAN GREEN

Grunewald & the Wannsee: Grandeur and Art

- Berlin Schloßhotel
- Brücke Museum
- Villa Liebermann

Lying southwest of Charlottenburg on the pleasant Havel lake, which meanders all the way to Potsdam, the affluent suburb of Grunewald has for centuries been home to local aristocracy, more recently to many foreign ambassadors. Perhaps the best way to experience the regal lifestyle vicariously is to stay at the grand Schloßhotel, formerly the von Pannwitz Palais. After two years of construction, the palace was completed in 1914 for Walter von Pannwitz and his wife, Catalina Roth. Both were socially renowned: he as a celebrity lawyer who counted Emperor Wilhelm II among his clients and she as a rich and glamorous Argentinean heiress twenty-two years his junior. An air of scandal hung about the von Pannwitzes, particularly when Roth became the mistress of the Emperor. Over a hundred visits were recorded by Wilhelm's steward to the house, many during von Pannwitz's travels to build his impressive art collection.

In 1991 the palace received a preservation order and a makeover from fashion designer Karl Lagerfeld. A stone spiral staircase leading up to Roth's boudoir – installed for and by the Emperor – is still a feature of the only original *Schloß* (castle) hotel in Berlin. The mix of the palace's original seigneurial décor with touches from Lagerfeld at the peak of his 1980s opulent Chanel period

BRÜCK
TEMPERATUREN
WASSER
LUFT

ensures the hotel's enduring allure. Lagerfeld converted Roth's own rooms into the Grunewald Suite (referred to as the 'Lagerfeld Suite'). With a spa and swimming pool, landscaped grounds, ballroom, period furniture and ornate walls and ceilings – practically no surface was left untouched – the hotel is the ultimate indulgence.

This verdant edge of Berlin has always been popular with artists. The seminal Expressionist movement Die Brücke (The Bridge) was formed by four men who met while studying architecture at Dresden. Fritz Bleyl, Erich Heckel, Ernst Ludwig Kirchner and Karl Schmidt-Rottluff formed the movement in 1905 and were later joined by Max Pechstein and Emil Nolde. Set amid mature pine and birch trees, the intimate Brücke Museum is a fitting location for a collection entirely dedicated to the group's naturalistic work, which comprises some 400 paintings and sculptures and several thousand drawings, watercolours and prints.

Wannsee lake, bordering Grunewald on the southwest, has also been the setting for artistic inspiration. Find your way to the waterfront house of painter Max Liebermann, leader of the New Realist movement and central figure of German Impressionism from the late 19th century until the 1930s. He acquired the country residence in 1909, commissioning Paul Baumgarten to build the house. For the garden he hired Albert Broderson and took horticultural advice from Alfred Lichtwark, known at the time for his reforming garden design. The resulting house and natural surroundings provided Liebermann with endless inspiration for the following two decades. Today the summer house also features works by other great Impressionists, such as Degas, Monet and Manet.

THE WORLD ACCORDING TO HISTORY

Potsdam: Prussian Magnificence

- Park Sanssouci
- Schloß Cecilienhof
- Villa Kellermann

A mere twelve miles (twenty kilometres) south-west of Berlin lies Potsdam, the capital of the Brandenburg region. It is so rich in history and unique examples of architecture of different periods that much of the town has been designated a UNESCO World Heritage site. The town centre, for example, is called the 'Holländisches Viertel' (Dutch Quarter), named by Friedrich Wilhelm I for immigrant Dutch workers he hoped to attract to build his palaces. Walking along the streets of low-storeyed, step-gabled houses you could be forgiven for thinking you're in the Netherlands.

Potsdam's green centrepiece is the magnificent Park Sanssouci (French for 'without care'), a 290-hectare (720-acre) playground of royal Germans. Beginning in 1744, Friedrich II designed Schloß Sanssouci himself, aided by his architect-friend Georg Wenzeslaus, as representation of his love for all things French. With its commanding position and Rococo ornamentation, the palace became a high palace of pleasure and culture, the ambience of which remains undiminished by time. Among the countless architectural treasures and follies in the park, do not miss Karl Friedrich Schinkel's delightful Schloß Charlottenburg, a comparatively modest but perfectly formed neoclassical house and garden that are fused into a unified whole.

Elsewhere in Potsdam, set within the Neuer Garten on the Havel Lake, is Schloß Cecilienhof, built to resemble a Tudor hunting lodge for Crown Prince Wilhelm in 1913. In 1945, the stately building played host to Truman, Stalin and Attlee as they signed a treaty that sentenced Germany to over four decades of division. Part of the palace has been converted into a hotel and restaurant, affording a glimpse into old royal life. For a rest from Potsdam's rich cultural and historical heritage, head to Bernhard Kellermann's Villa Kellermann, a mansion set on a green lawn overlooking the water. He serves Italian and German cuisine in idyllic surroundings on a lake that brings together the city's many parks.

THE WHITE CITY

Heiligendamm: Seaside Spa Style

• Grand Hotel Heiligendamm

The first German oceanside spa was established at Heiligendamm, on a stretch of beach between beech woodlands and the Baltic Sea. In 1793 sea bathing was a recreation for 'mad dogs and Englishmen' only, but Duke Friedrich Franz I of Mecklenburg–Schwerin, acting on doctor's orders, decided to give it a try. Plunge pools and all other amenities and ideas associated with wellness have been close to the lifestyle of Germans ever since. Heiligendamm, where Friedrich made his initial splash, became the society beach of choice. His bouncing steps from Kurhaus to ocean have been followed by Marcel Proust, Felix Mendelssohn-Bartholdy, Queen Luise of Prussia and Tsar Nicholas I. The regal presence explains the grandeur of a collection of houses referred to as 'The White City'. All of them are protected monuments, and some seven make up the Kempinski Grand Hotel Heiligendamm complex, which opened in 2003.

The site was in former East Germany, and during the 1950s had been a workers' sanatorium. It took the contemporary influence of Anna Marie Jagdfeld, who, with her property magnate husband, has become a familiar name in Berlin and is behind the fashion boutique Quartier 206 and the Adlon hotel complex (p. 112), which includes Restaurant Felix and the China Club. Making each of the rooms and suites different but united by calm beige, blue and sand tones to reflect the coastal location, she transformed the houses into one of the most exclusive resorts in Europe. Jagdfeld worked on six of the houses and a children's crèche, the result is a cocoon of health, spa and comfort. The only new building in the grounds, the Severin Palace, features ground and lower-ground floors dedicated to physical well-being. A huge sauna, ceiling dotted with fairy-lights emulating a starlit sky, an ice-room, a colour-mood-coordinated caldarium, steam baths, hammam and swimming pool with massage pumps and jacuzzi, plus the full repertoire of beauty treatments ensure that Heiligendamm will remain a timeless seaside retreat for generations to come.

QUINTESSENTIALLY SO

Quedlinburg: Medieval Magic

• Romantik Hotel Theophano

Time has stood still since the early 1300s in this town that nestles in the shadow of the Harz mountains. Originating from a 10th-century abbey founded by Otto I and lying on a vital trading corridor during the Middle Ages ('the secret capital of the Romanesque Road'), Quedlinburg remained physically unscathed by world wars and Communist demolition plans. In 1994 its 1600 half-timbered houses and church were listed as UNESCO World Heritage sites. For over seven centuries they have survived en masse, and the town is as authentically German as modern life will allow.

Quedlinburg was founded as a township when Saxon Duke Heinrich chose it as the location for his coronation as the first Saxon king of Germany. So followed the politics and intrigue of Imperial life, and for the next two centuries Quedlinburg was one of the de rigueur seasonal abodes of the travelling aristocracy. The old town square, museums and houses reflect a regal past, most cheek-by-jowl along winding cobbled alleyways and ominously overlooked by the town's Romanesque masterpiece, the Collegiate Church of St Servatius situated atop the Schloßberg (Castle Hill). Although its architecture and the objects in its treasury are celebrated nationwide, it was once used for dubious purposes during the Nazi regime under Heinrich Himmler, who turned it into a shrine to his belief that Heinrich I was the founder of the German Reich.

The town still bursts with civic pride, cleanliness and care, and characterful shops and establishments abound. For lodging, try the Romantik Hotel Theophano, a large merchant's house built in 1668 on the market square and later seat of the Tanner's Guild. A hotel since 1900, it features a linen shop and *gemütlich* sandstone-vaulted restaurant serving such local specialties as wild boar and Harz trout.

contact

All telephone numbers are given for dialling locally: the country code for Germany is +49; the code for Berlin is 030. Calling from abroad one dials (+49 30) followed by the number given. Telephone numbers in the retreat section are given for dialling from Berlin.
The number in brackets by the name is the page number on which the entry appears.

Abendmahl [64]
Muskauer Straße 9
10997 Berlin
T 6 12 51 70
F 69 53 47 32
E abendmahl@abendmahl-berlin.de
W www.abendmahl-berlin.de

Absinth Depot Berlin [32]
Weinmeisterstraße 4
10178 Berlin
T 2 81 67 89

adidas Originals Store [160]
Münzstraße 13–15
10178 Berlin
T 27 59 43 81
F 27 59 43 83
W www.adidas.com/de

Aigner [38]
Am Gendarmenmarkt
Charlottenstraße 50–52
10117 Berlin
T 20 37 51 85 0
W www.aigner-gendarmenmarkt.de

Alte Nationalgalerie [17]
Bodestraße 1–3
10178 Berlin
T 20 90 58 01
F 20 90 58 02
E ang@smb.spk-berlin.de
W www.smb.spk-berlin.de

Altes Museum [17]
Am Kupfergraben
10178 Berlin
T 20 90 52 01
F 20 90 52 02
E ant@smb.spk-berlin.de
W www.smb.spk-berlin.de

Alt-Luxemburg [135]
Windscheidstraße 31
10627 Berlin
T 3 23 87 30
F 3 27 40 03
E info@altluxemburg.de
W www.altluxemburg.de

Anastasia [72]
Samariterstraße 13
10247 Berlin
T 41 72 48 99

April [81]
Winterfeldtstraße 56
10781 Berlin
T 2 16 88 69

Aquamarin [65]
Bergmannstraße 20
10961 Berlin
T 6 93 34 40

Aquarium [78]
Budapester Straße 32
10787 Berlin
W www.aquarium-berlin.de

Art + Industry [95]
Bleibtreustraße 40
10623 Berlin
T 8 83 49 46
F 88 72 96 70
W www.artindustryberlin.de

Bar [17]
Karl-Marx-Allee 36
10178 Berlin

Bar Jeder Vernunft [98]
Schaperstraße 24
10719 Berlin
T 8 83 15 82
W www.bar-jeder-vernunft.de

Bateau Ivre [68]
Oranienstraße 18
10999 Berlin
T 61 40 36 59
F 6 15 37 01

Berliner Ensemble [36]
Theater am Schiffbauerdamm
Bertolt Brecht Platz 1
10117 Berlin
T 28 40 80
W www.berliner-ensemble.de

Berliner Fernsehturm [17]
Alexanderplatz
10178 Berlin
T 2 42 33 33
F 2 42 59 22
E info@berlinerfernsehturm.de
W www.berlinerfernsehturm.de

Berlinische Galerie [63]
Alte Jakobstraße 124–28
10969 Berlin
T 78 90 26 00
F 78 90 27 01
E bg@berlinischegalerie.de
W www.berlinischergalerie.de

Berlinomat [167]
Frankfurter Allee 89
10247 Berlin
T 42 08 14 45
E info@berlinomat.com
W www.berlinomat.com

Beth Café [32]
Tucholskystraße 40
10117 Berlin
T 2 81 31 35

Biscotti [103]
Pestalozzistraße 88
10625 Berlin
T 3 12 39 37

Blush [24]
Rosa-Luxemburg-Straße 22
10178 Berlin
T 28 09 35 80
F 28 09 35 81
W www.blush-berlin.com

BonBon Macherei [27]
Heckmann Höfe
Oranienburger Straße 32
10117 Berlin
T 44 05 52 43
W www.bonbonmacherei.de

Breathe [163]
Rochstraße 17
10178 Berlin
T 24 34 25 77
F 24 34 25 78
E welcome@breathe-cosmetics.com
W www.breathe-cosmetics.com

Brille 54 [28]
Rosenthaler Straße 36
Rosenhöfe
10178 Berlin
T 28 04 08 18
W www.brille54.de

Brot und Rosen [139]
Am Friedrichshain 6
10407 Berlin
T 4 23 19 16

Bücherbogen [101]
Savignyplatz
Stadtbahnbogen 593
10623 Berlin
T 31 86 95 11
F 3 13 72 37
E savignyplatz@buecherbogen.com
W www.buecherbogen.com

Café Adler [129]
Friedrichstraße 206
10969 Berlin
T 2 51 89 65

Café am Neuen See [145]
Lichtensteinallee 2
10787 Berlin
T 2 54 49 30
F 25 44 93 33
E info@cafeamneuensee.de
W www.cafeamneuensee.de

Café am Ufer [63]
Paul-Lincke-Ufer 42
10999 Berlin
T 61 62 92 00
F 61 62 92 06
E mail@cafe-am-ufer.de
W www.cafe-am-ufer.de

Café Einstein [83]
Kurfürstenstraße 58
10785 Berlin
T 2 61 50 96
F 2 61 91 76
E contact@cafeeinstein.com
W www.cafeeinstein.com

Café Morgenland [63]
Skalitzer Straße 35
10999 Berlin
T 61 13 29 17

Café Savigny [101]
Grolmanstraße 53
10623 Berlin
T 3 12 81 95

Café Schönbrunn [72]
Am Schwanenteich, Volkspark Friedrichshain
10407 Berlin
T 42 02 81 91

Cantian [46]
Cantianstraße 11
10437 Berlin
T 13 89 20 04

Cara Tonga [163]
Dircksenstraße 51
10178 Berlin
T 28 38 91 61

Chapeaux [96]
Bleibtreustraße 51
10623 Berlin
T 3 12 09 13

Chocolaterie Estrellas [170]
Akazienstraße 21
10823 Berlin
T 78 95 66 46

Claudia Skoda [164]
Alte Schönhauser Straße 35
10119 Berlin
T 2 80 72 11
F 28 39 01 78
E contact@claudiaskoda.com
W www.claudiaskoda.com

Club 12/34 [154]
Fritz Fischer, Stralauer Allee 1
10245 Berlin
T 5 20 07 23 01
F 5 20 07 23 43
E info@club1234.de
W www.club1234.de

Cookies [38]
Charlottenstraße 42
10117 Berlin
W www.cookies.ch

Cookies Cream [38]
Charlottenstraße 45
10117 Berlin
T 20 91 27 27
W www.cookies-cream.de

Cream [144]
Schlesische Straße 6
10997 Berlin
T 61 07 49 80
W www.cream-berlin.de

CSA Bar [155]
Karl-Marx-Allee 96
10243 Berlin
T 29 04 47 41

Dachgarten [137]
Reichstag, Platz der Republik 1
11011 Berlin
T 22 62 99 33
F 22 62 99 43

Deutsches Historisches Museum [17]
Unter den Linden 2
10117 Berlin
T 20 30 40
F 20 30 45 43
W www.dhm.de

Diener Tatterssall [149]
Grolmanstraße 47
10623 Berlin
T 8 81 53 29

Die Imaginäre Manufaktur (DIM) [173]
Oranienstraße 26
10999 Berlin
T 9 02 98 66 12
F 9 02 98 66 15
E info@blindenanstalt.de
W www.blindenanstalt.de

Digalittledeeper [18]
Torstraße 102
10119 Berlin
T 97 00 51 06
E contact@digalittledeeper.net
W www.digalittledeeper.net

Dorint am Gendarmenmarkt [114]
Charlottenstraße 50–52
10117 Berlin
T 20 37 50
F 20 37 51 00
W www.dorint.de

Eigen + Art [27]
Auguststraße 26
10117 Berlin
T 2 80 66 05
F 2 80 66 16
E berlin@eigen-art.com
W www.eigen-art.com

Eisdieler [46]
Kastanienallee 12
10435 Berlin
T 2 85 73 51
W www.eisdieler.de

Engelbecken [103]
Witzlebenstraße 31
14057 Berlin
T 6 15 28 10
W www.engelbecken.de

Engelbrecht [139]
Schiffbauerdamm 6/7
10117 Berlin
T 28 59 85 85
F 28 59 85 87
E info@engelbrecht-berlin.de
W www.engelbrecht-berlin.de

Enoiteca Il Calice [95]
Walter-Benjamin-Platz 4
10629 Berlin
T 3 24 23 08
W www.enoiteca-il-calice.de

Exil Wohnmagazin [55]
Backfabrik
Prenzlauer Allee 250
10405 Berlin
T 44 35 09 30
F 44 35 09 39
W www.exil-wohnmagazin.de

Facil [140]
Potsdamer Straße 3
10785 Berlin
T 5 90 05 12 34
F 5 90 05 22 22
W www.facil-berlin.de

Fadeninsel [68]
Oranienstraße 23
10999 Berlin
T 6 15 69 94
W www.fadeninsel.de

Felsenkeller [146]
Akazienstraße 2
10823 Berlin
T 7 81 34 47

Fiebelkorn & Kuckuck [98]
Bleibtreustraße 4
10623 Berlin
Kuckuck:
T 31 50 71 50
Fiebelkorn:
T 3 12 33 73
F 31 50 71 50

Fiona Bennett [162]
Große Hamburger Straße 25
10110 Berlin
T 28 09 63 30
E info@fionabennett.com
W www.fionabennett.com

Florian [138]
Grolmanstraße 52
10623 Berlin

T 3 13 91 84
F 3 12 39 75
E florian.berlin@t-online.de
W www.gastro-lloyd.de

Der Freischwimmer [71]
Vor dem Schlesischen Tor 2a
10997 Berlin
T 61 07 43 09
E pool@freischwimmer-berlin.de
W www.freischwimmer-berlin.de

Gainsbourg [148]
Savignyplatz 5
10623 Berlin
T 3 13 74 64
F 3 13 88 00
W www.gainsbourg.de

Galerie Aedes [101]
Savignyplatz, Bogen 600–1
10623 Berlin
T 2 82 70 15
W www.aedes-galerie.de

Galerie Bremer [153]
Fasanenstraße 37
10719 Berlin
T 8 81 49 08

Galerie Tagebau [35]
Rosenthaler Straße 19
10119 Berlin
T 28 38 48 69

Galerie 2000 [98]
Knesebeckstraße 56–58
10719 Berlin
T 8 83 84 67

Gallery / Shop [32]
Neue Schönhauser Straße 19
10178 Berlin
T 28 09 92 92
F 28 09 92 94
W www.neue-schoenhauser-19.de

GB [30]
Auguststraße 77–78
10178 Berlin
T 28 39 01 03

Gorgonzola Club [151]
Dresdener Straße 121
10997 Berlin
T 6 15 64 73

Gottlob [80]
Akazienstraße 17
10827 Berlin
T 78 70 80 95

Green Door [148]
Winterfeldtstraße 50
10781 Berlin
T 2 15 25 15
F 2 15 34 06
E contact@greendoor.de
W www.greendoor.de

Gugelhof [50]
Knaackstraße 37
10435 Berlin
T 4 42 92 29
F 44 35 95 40
E gugelhof@t-online.de
W www.gugelhof.de

Hackbarth's [30]
Auguststraße 49a
10119 Berlin
T 2 82 77 06
F 28 09 77 10

Hamburger Bahnhof [36]
Invalidenstraße 50–51
10557 Berlin
T 39 78 34 11
W www.hamburgerbahnof.de

Hasipop [49]
Oderberger Straße 39
10435 Berlin
T 44 03 34 91
E hasipop@hasipop.de
W www.hasipop.de

Hasir [27]
Oranienburger Straße 4
10997 Berlin
T 28 04 16 16
E info@hasir.de
W www.hasir.de

Hebbel-Theater [65]
Stresemannstraße 29
10963 Berlin
T 2 59 00 40
F 25 90 04 49
W www.hebbel-theater.de

Herr von Eden [21]
Alte Schönhauser Straße 20
10119 Berlin
T 24 04 86 82
W www.herrvoneden.de

Herz und Stöhr [81]
Winterfeldtstraße 52
10781 Berlin
T 2 16 44 25
W www.herz-stoehr.de

Holly [24]
Alte Schönhauser Straße 4
10119 Berlin
T 97 89 49 94
E contact@holly-berlin.de
W www.holly-berlin.de

Honigmond Garden Hotel [108]
Invalidenstraße 112
10115 Berlin
T 28 44 55 77
F 28 44 55 88
E honigmond@t-online.de
W www.honigmond-berlin.de

Hotel Adlon Kempinski [112]
Unter den Linden 77
10117 Berlin
T 22 61 0
F 22 61 22 22
E adlon@kempinski.com
W www.hotel-adlon.de

Hotel Bleibtreu [93]
Bleibtreustraße 31
10707 Berlin
T 88 47 40
F 88 47 44 44
E info@bleibtreu.com
W www.bleibtreu.com

Hotel Brandenburger Hof [122]
Eislebener Straße 14
10789 Berlin
T 21 40 50
F 21 40 51 00
E info@brandenburger-hof.com
W www.brandenburger-hof.com

Hugos [136]
Hotel Intercontinental
Budapester Straße 2
10787 Berlin
T 26 02 12 63
F 26 02 12 39
E mail@hugos-restaurant.de
W www.hugos-restaurant.de

Hut Up [166]
Oranienburger Straße 32
10117 Berlin
T 28 38 61 05
F 28 38 61 06
E info@hutup.de
W www.hutup.de

In't Veld Schokoladen [171]
Dunckerstraße 10
10437 Berlin
T 48 62 34 23
W www.intveld.de

Iskele [63]
Gegenüber Planufer 82
10967 Berlin
T 69 50 72 65

Jüdisches Museum [60]
Lindenstraße 9–14
10969 Berlin
T 25 99 33 00
E info@jmberlin.de
W www.jmberlin.de

Jules Vernes [90]
Schlüterstraße 61
10625 Berlin
T 31 80 94 10

KaDeWe [169]
Tauentzienstraße 21–24
10789 Berlin
T 21 21 0
E info@kadewe.de
W www.kadewe.de

Kaffee Burger [18]
Torstraße 60
10119 Berlin
E tanzwirtschaft@kaffeeburger.de
W www.kaffeeburger.de

Kafka [68]
Oranienstraße 204
10999 Berlin
T 6 12 24 29
E restaurant.kafka@gmx.de
W www.restaurant-kafka.de

Kaisersaal [41]
Bellevuestraße 1
10785 Berlin
T 25 75 14 54
F 25 75 14 56
E info@kaisersaal-berlin.de
W www.kaisersaal-berlin.de

Käthe-Kollwitz-Museum [93]
Fasanenstraße 24
T 8 82 52 10
F 8 81 19 01
E info@kaethe-kollwitz.de
W www.kaethe-kollwitz.de

Kaufhaus Schrill [95]
Bleibtreustraße 46
10623 Berlin
T 8 82 40 48
F 88 55 20 45
E schrill@snafu.de
W www.schrill.de

Klemkes Wein- und Spezialitäteneck [95]
Mommsenstraße 9
10629 Berlin
T 88 55 12 60
F 8 83 12 29

Knofi [64]
Bergmannstraße 98
10961 Berlin
T 6 94 58 07

Kochlust [22]
Alte Schönhauser Straße 36/37
10119 Berlin
T 24 63 88 83
F 24 63 88 85
E info@kochlust-berlin.de
W www.kochlust-berlin.de

Kollhoff Building [41]
Potsdamer Platz 1
10785 Berlin
T 25 29 43 72
W www.panoramapunkt.de

KPM [36]
Unter den Linden 35
10117 Berlin
T 2 06 41 50
E unterdenlinden@kpm-berlin.de
W www.kpm-berlin.de

Ku'damm 101 [124]
Kurfürstendamm 101
10711 Berlin
T 5 20 05 50
F 5 20 05 55 55
E info@kudamm101.com
W www.kudamm101.com

Kulturbrauerei [49]
Schönhauser Allee 36–39
10435 Berlin
T 44 35 26 0
W www.kulturbrauerei.de

Kumpelnest 3000 [152]
Lützowstraße 23
10785 Berlin
T 2 61 69 18

Kunst-Werke Berlin [29]
Auguststraße 69
10117 Berlin
T 28 04 49 03
F 28 04 49 03
W www.kw-berlin.de

Liquidrom at the Tempodrom [67]
Möckernstraße 10
10963 Berlin
T 74 73 71 71
E info@liquidrom.com
W www.liquidrom.com

Lisa D. [29]
Hackesche Höfe
Rosenthalerstraße 40–41
10178 Berlin
T 2 83 43 54
W www.lisad.com

Literaturhaus [90]
Fasanenstraße 23
10179 Berlin
T 8 87 28 60;
café: 8 82 34 14
E literaturhaus@berlin.de
W www.literaturahus-berlin.de

Lubitsch [138]
Bleibtreustraße 47
10623 Berlin
T 8 82 37 56
F 8 85 12 94

Lucid 21 [68]
Mariannenstraße 50
10997 Berlin
T 69 51 50 20
E bambi@lucid21.net
W www.lucid21.net

Luise: Hotel + Kunstlerheim [110]
Luisenstraße 19
T 28 44 80
F 28 44 84 48
E info@kuenstlerheim-luise.de
W www.kuenstlerheim-luise.de

Lutter und Wegner [130]
Schlüterstraße 55
10629 Berlin
T 8 81 34 40
F 8 81 92 56
E lutterundwegner@gmx.de
W www.restaurant lutterundwegner.de

Madison [116]
Potsdamer Straße 3
10785 Berlin
T 5 90 05 00 00
F 5 90 0505 40
E welcome@madison-berlin.de
W www.madison-berlin.de

Malatesta [36]
Charlottenstraße 59
10117 Berlin
T 20 94 50 71
E mail@ristorante-malatesta.de
W www.ristorante-malatesta.de

Mao Thai [51]
Wörther Straße 30
10405 Berlin
T 4 41 92 61
F 44 34 20 90
W www.thaipage.com

Marietta [55]
Stargarder Straße 13
10437 Berlin
T 43 72 06 46
E info@marietta-bar.de
W www.marietta-bar.de

Martin Gropius Bau [60]
Niederkirchnerstraße 7/
Stresemannstraße 110
10663 Berlin
T 25 48 60
W www.gropiusbau.de

Maxwell [133]
Bergstraße 22
10115 Berlin
T 2 80 71 21
F 28 59 98 48
E maxwell.berlin@t-online.de
W www.verybest.de/maxwell

Melanie [171]
Goethestraße 4
10623 Berlin
T 3 13 83 30

Menardie [38]
Alt Moabit 143–45
10557 Berlin
T 3 94 05 10
W www.menardie.de

Morena [71]
Wiener Straße 60
10999 Berlin
T 6 11 35 78
F 6 18 35 45
W www.morena-berlin.de

Museum für Fotographie [98]
Jebensstraße 2
10623 Berlin
T 20 90 55 66

Mutabilis [52]
Stubbenkammerstraße 4
10437 Berlin
T 44 79 38 16
F 44 67 85 01
E info@mutabilis.de
W www.mutabilis.de

Neue Nationalgalerie [41]
Potsdamer Straße 50
10785 Berlin
T 2 66 26 51
F 2 62 47 15
E nng@smb.spk-berlin.de
W www.smb.spk-berlin.de/nng

Neues Kranzler Eck [96]
Kurfürstendamm
10719 Berlin
W www.neueskranzlereck.de

Newton Bar [157]
Charlottenstraße 57
10117 Berlin
T 20 61 29 99
F 20 29 54 25
W www.newton-bar.de

90 Grad [83]
Dennewitzstraße 37
10785 Berlin
T 27 59 62 31
W www.90grad.com

Nix [165]
Heckmannhöfe,
Oranienburger Straße 32
10117 Berlin
T 2 81 80 44
F 28 38 55 77
W www.nix.de

Nocti Vagus [55]
Saarbrücker Straße 36–38
10405 Berlin
T 74 74 91 23
F 44 34 12 75
E kontakt@noctivagus.de
W www.noctivagus.de

Nola's Am Weinberg [18]
Veteranenstraße 9
10119 Berlin
T 44 04 07 66
E info@nola.de
W www.nola.de

Ottenthal [134]
Kantstraße 153
10623 Berlin
T 3 13 31 62
F 3 13 37 32
E ottenthal-restaurant@t-online.de
W www.ottenthal.de

Paris Bar [131]
Kantstraße 152
10623 Berlin
T 3 13 80 52
F 3 13 28 16
W www.parisbar.de

Pasternak [150]
Knaackstraße 22–24
10405 Berlin
T 4 41 33 99
F 4 41 33 99
E info@restaurant-pasternak.de
W www.restaurant-pasternak.de

Patrick Hellmann [93]
Fasanenstraße 28 & 29
10719 Berlin
T 88 48 77 15 / 8 81 19 85
E info@patrickhellmann.com
W www.patrickhellmann.com

Penthesileia [35]
Tucholskystraße 31
10117 Berlin
T 2 82 11 52
W www.penthesileia.de

Pergamonmuseum [17]
Am Kupfergraben
10178 Berlin
T 20 90 55 66
W www.smb.spk-berlin.de

Pfefferberg [46]
Fehrbelliner Straße 92
10119 Berlin
W www.pfefferberg.de

Philharmonie [41]
Potsdamer Straße 33
10772 Berlin
T 25 48 89 99
W www.berliner-philharmoniker.de

Prater Garten & Hecht Club [147]
Kastanienallee 7–9
10435 Berlin
T 4 48 56 88
F 44 34 09 04
W www.pratergarten.de

Pro QM [172]
Alte Schönhauser Straße 48
10119 Berlin
T 24 72 85 20
F 24 72 85 21
E info@pro-qm.de
W www.pro-qm.de

Propeller Island City Lodge [118]
Albrecht-Achilles-Straße 58
10709 Berlin
T 8 91 90 16
F 8 92 87 21
W www.propeller-island.com

Q! [120]
Knesebeckstraße 67
10623 Berlin
T 81 00 66 0
F 81 00 66 666
E q-berlin@loock-hotels.com
W www.q-berlin.de

Qiu [157]
Potsdamer Straße 3
10785 Berlin
T 59 00 00 00
W www.qiu.de

Q3A [154]
Stralauer Allee 2c
10245 Berlin
T 29 35 29 14
F 29 35 21 40
E info@q3a-berlin.de
W www.q3a-berlin.de

Re-Store [35]
Auguststraße 3
10117 Berlin
T 28 09 58 42
E info@re-store.de
W www.re-store.de

Revanche de la Femme [96]
Uhlandstraße 50
10719 Berln
T 88 91 26 72
W www.revanchedelafemme.de

Rio [96]
Bleibtreustraße 52
10623 Berlin
T 3 13 31 52
F 3 12 33 85
E rio-schmuck@t-online.de

Riva [30]
Dircksenstraße, bogen 142
10178 Berlin
T 24 72 26 88
W www.riva-berlin.de

RoomSafari [49]
Swinemünder Straße 6
10435 Berlin
T 44 30 82 95
E welcome@roomsafari.com
W www.roomsafari.com

Rote Harfe/ Orient Lounge [153]
Oranienstraße 13
10999 Berlin
T 6 18 44 46

RSVP Papier in Mitte [172]
Mulackstraße 14
10119 Berlin
T 28 09 46 44
W www.moleskine.de

RumTrader [93]
Fasanenstraße 40
10719 Berlin
T 8 81 14 28

Sabine Kniesche [52]
Knaackstraße 33
10405 Berlin
T 40 50 04 05
W www.sabinekniesche.de

Sale e Tabacci [141]
Kochstraße 18
10969 Berlin
T 2 52 11 55
F 25 29 50 04
E saleetabacchi@aol.com
W www.gourmetguide.com/saleetabacchi

Sammlung DaimlerChrysler [38]
Haus Huth
Potsdamer Straße 5
10785 Berlin
W www.sammlung.daimlerchrysler.com

Sammlung Hoffmann [23]
Sophie-Gips-Höfe
Sophienstraße 21
10178 Berlin
T 28 49 91 21
E sammlung@sophie-gips.de
W www.sophie-gips.de

Saunabad [52]
Rykestraße 10
10405 Berlin
T 44 04 63 97
W www.saunabad-berlin.de

Schaubühne am Lehniner Platz [103]
Kurfürstendamm 153
10709 Berlin
T 89 00 20
F 8 90 02 190
E ticket@schaubuehne.de
W www.schaubuehne.de

Schelpmeier [52]
Knaackstraße 20a
10405 Berlin
T 39 10 24 20

Schloß Charlottenburg [103]
Spandauer Damm 20–24
14059 Berlin
T 32 09 14 40
W www.spsg.de

Schokoladenfabrik [68]
Mariannenstraße 6
10997 Berlin
T 6 15 14 64
W www.schokofabrik.de

Schuhtanten [63]
Paul-Lincke-Ufer 44
10999 Berlin
T 61 62 97 56
E info@schuhtanten.de
W www.schuhtanten.de

Schwarzenraben [22]
Neue Schönhauser Straße 13
10178 Berlin
T 28 39 16 98
F 28 39 16 97
E info@schwarzenraben.de
W www.schwarzenraben.de

Shima [78]
Schwäbische Straße 5
10781 Berlin
T 2 11 19 90
E info@shima-world.de
W www.shima-world.de

Sony Center [38]
Potsdamer Platz
10785 Berlin
T 25 75 57 58
W www.sonycenter.de

Sophiensaele [24]
Sophienstraße 18
10178 Berlin
T 27 89 00 30
F 2 83 52 67
E info@sophiensaele.com
W www.sophiensaele.de

Stilwerk [96]
Kantstraße 17
10623 Berlin
T 31 51 55 00
E berlin@stilwerk.de
W www.stilwerk.de

Storch [134]
Wartburgstraße 54
10823 Berlin
T/F 7 84 20 59
E hauptvogel@storch-berlin.de
W www.storch-berlin.de

Strandbad [49]
Kollwitzplatz
Wörther Straße 12
10435 Berlin
T 70 72 79 22

Südwind [80]
Akazienstraße 7
10823 Berlin
T 7 82 04 39
F 78 71 86 83
W www.suedwind.net

suitcasearchitecture [49]
Choriner Straße 54
10435 Berlin
T 44 04 59 33
E berlin@suitcasearchitecture.com
W www.suitcasearchitecture.de

Tacheles [36]
Oranienburger Straße 54–56
10117 Berlin
W www.tacheles.de

Tadschikische Teestube & Die Möwe [145]
Palais am Festungsgraben
Am Festungsgraben 1
10117 Berlin
T 20 61 05 40
F 20 61 05 50
E info@restaurant-moewe.de
W www.restaurant-moewe.de

TaschenDesign Accessoires [21]
Torstraße 97
10119 Berlin
T 4 40 29 91
E moniaherbst@bywerk.de
W www.moniaherbst.de

Thatchers [28]
Hackesche Höfe
Rosenthaler Straße 40–41
10178 Berlin
T 27 58 22 10
W www.thatchers.de

Topographie des Terrors [60]
Niederkirchnerstraße 8
10963 Berlin
T 25 48 67 03
W www.topographie.de

Tosh [52]
Sredzkistraße 56
10405 Berlin
T 44 03 83 50
F 44 03 83 51

E info@tosh.de
W www.tosh.de

Trippen [161]
Hackesche Höfe
Rosenthaler Straße 40–41
10178 Berlin
T 28 39 13 37
E info@trippen.com
W www.trippen-shoes.com

Universum Lounge [103]
Kurfürstendamm 153
10709 Berlin
T 89 06 49 94
F 32 76 47 95

Unsicht-Bar Berlin [32]
Gormannstraße 14
10119 Berlin
T 24 34 25 00
F 24 34 25 01
W www.unsicht-bar-berlin.de

Victoria Bar [83]
Potsdamer Straße 102
10785 Berlin
T 25 75 99 77
W www.victoriabar.de

Vielspiel [27]
Große Hamburger Straße 28
10110 Berlin
T 96 06 52 66
W www.vielspiel.de

Volksbühne: Roter and Grüner Salon [156]
Rosa-Luxemburg-Platz
10178 Berlin
Roter Salon
T 24 06 58 06
E info@roter-salon.de
W www.roter-salon.de
Grüner Salon:
T 28 59 89 36
W www.gruener-salon.de

VorOrt [24]
Alte Schönhauser Straße 47
10119 Berlin
T 24 72 47 31

Watergate [144]
Falckensteinstraße 49
10997 Berlin
T 61 28 03 94
W www.water-gate.de

Weinerei [168]
Veteranenstraße 14
10119 Berlin
T/F 4 40 69 83
E info@weinerei.com
W www.weinerei.com

Weinguy [128]
Luisenstraße 19
10117 Berlin
T 28 09 84 84
F 28 09 84 74
E info@weinguy.de
W www.weinguy.de

Weinhandlung Baumgart & Braun [50]
Wörther Straße 21
10405 Berlin
T 4 41 02 35

Weinrestaurant Risachér [101]
Savignyplatz 11
10623 Berlin
T 3 13 86 97
F 31 80 07 60

Weinrot [132]
Savoy Hotel
Fasanenstraße 9–10
10623 Berlin
T 31 10 30
F 31 10 33 33
E info@savoy-hotel.com
W www.hotel-savoy.com

Whisky and Cigars [168]
Sophienstraße 23
10178 Berlin
T 2 82 03 76
F 2 82 03 76
E laden@whisky-cigars.de
W www.whisky-cigars.de

Wohnmaschine [23]
Tucholskystraße 35
10117 Berlin
T 30 87 20 15
F 30 87 20 16
E info@wohnmaschine.de
W www.wohnmaschine.de

Wohnzimmer [55]
Lettestraße 6
10405 Berlin
T 4 45 54 58

WMF [18]
Karl-Marx Allee /
Schillingstraße
10178 Berlin
T 2 88 78 89 10
F 2 88 78 89 88
E info@wmfclub.de
W www.wmfclub.de

Würgeengel [151]
Dresdener Straße 122
10997 Berlin
T 6 15 55 60

Württemberger Weinhaus [96]
Kantstraße/Neues Kranzlereck
Im Stadtbahnbogen 547
10623 Berlin
T 37 59 22 93
F 37 59 22 95

Yoshiharu Ito [27]
Auguststraße 19
10117 Berlin
T 44 04 44 90
E contact@itofashion.com
W www.yoshiharu-ito.de

Zigarren Herzog [95]
Ludwigkirchplatz 1
10719 Berlin
T 88 68 23 40
F 88 68 23 42
E info@zigarren-herzog.com
W www.zigarren-herzog.com

GRUNEWALD & THE WANNSEE [176]

Grunewald can be reached by S-Bahn line S7 from all main S-Bahn stations on the thick 'spine' through the city, including Alexanderplatz, Friedrichstraße and Zoologischer Garten (30 minutes). By car it can be reached by using the Hohenzollerndamm, which eventually runs into Clayallee, taking you directly to Grunewald. If you come from the Autobahn get off at Kurfürstendamm and take a right in the directrion of Königsweg (30 minutes).

Schloßhotel Berlin
Brahmsstraße 10
14193 Berlin
T (030) 89 58 40
F (030) 89 58 48 00
E info@schlosshotelberlin.com
W www.schlosshotelberlin.com

Brücke Museum
Bussardsteig 9
14195 Berlin-Dahlem
T (030) 8 31 20 29
F (030) 8 31 59 61
E bruecke-museum@t-online.de
W www.bruecke-museum.de

Villa Liebermann
Am Großen Wannsee 42
(entrance: Colomier Straße 3)
14109 Berlin
T (030) 80 58 38 30
F (030) 80 58 38 32
E info@liebermann-villa.de
W www.liebermann-villa.de

POTSDAM [180]

Take S-Bahn S1 (from Potsdamer Platz) or S7 (Zoologischer Garten and other main stations) to Potsdam. They run appoximately every 10 minutes and take 45 minutes. By car drive down Clayallee and turn right at the sign when Clayallee meets Potsdamer Chaussee. Follow all the way (incredibly beautiful) to Glienicker Brücke, (bridge), cross it and you are in Potsdam. The exit to the city is at Königstraße and the exit name is Potsdam (45 minutes)

Park Sanssouci
Potsdam
T (03 31) 96 94 202
W www.park-sanssouci.de

Schloß Cecilienhof
Neuer Garten
14414 Potsdam
T (03 31) 96 94 200 /201

Villa Kellermann
Mangerstraße 34–36
14467 Potsdam
T (03 31) 29 15 72
F (03 31) 28 03 738
W www.villa-kellermann.de

HEILIGENDAMM [182]

There are no direct trains from Berlin; it takes 3–5 hours with changes. By car take the Autobahn to Rostock and follow signs to Heiligendamm (approximately 2½ hours).

Grand Hotel Heiligendamm
18209 Heiligendamm
T (03 82 03) 7 40 0
F (03 82 03) 7 40 74 74
E reservations.heiligendamm@kempinski.com
W www.kempinski-heiligendamm.com

QUEDLINBURG [184]

By car take the Autobahn to Magdeburg, get off at Magdeburg-Sudenburg and follow signs. (approximately 3 hours).There are direct trains to Quedlinburg from Zoologischer Garten approximately every hour. (2½ hours) .

Romantik Hotel Theophano
Markt 13–14
06484 Quedlinburg
T (0 39 46) 96 30 0
F (0 39 46) 96 30 36
E theophano@t-online.de
W www.hoteltheophano.de